SCRAP SAVER'S
Bazaar
Stitchery

Sandra Lounsbury Foose

Oxmoor House, Inc.
Book Division of Southern Progress Corporation
P.O. Box 832463
Birmingham, AL 35201

Library of Congress Catalog Number: 90-61074
ISBN: 0-8487-0753-2
Manufactured in the United States of America
First Printing 1990

Executive Editor: Nancy J. Fitzpatrick
Production Manager: Jerry Higdon
Associate Production Manager: Rick Litton
Art Director: Bob Nance
Copy Chief: Mary Jean Haddin

Scrap Saver's Bazaar Stitchery

Editor: Susan Ramey Wright
Designer and photo stylist: Connie Formby
Editorial Assistant: Lelia Gray Neil
Copy Assistant: Susan Smith Cheatham
Production Assistant: Theresa L. Beste
Photographer: Colleen Duffley
Additional Photography: John O'Hagan, Melissa Springer

To find out how you can order *Cooking Light* magazine, write to *Cooking Light*®, P.O. Box C-549, Birmingham, AL 35283.

For my sister, Joyce.

♥

Sandy

CONTENTS

RAFFLE PRIZE

SUPPLIES AND TECHNIQUES

BAZAAR TODAY!

Whether posted on a country church green, a small-town square, or an urban schoolyard fence, the "Bazaar Today!" sign is definitely a traffic-stopping proclamation.

You are warmly welcomed to this bazaar-in-a-book! Just turn the page to open the door to a friendly place where ideas are shared and creativity is encouraged.

Go straight to Gifts Galore and select a few quick-and-easy projects. Check into the Children's Corner for some brand-new ideas for little ones. Visit the Christmas House for yuletide inspirations. But save time for a peek into the Holiday Fair section. It's filled with year-round, special-occasion designs.

You'll find that most of my bazaar projects are easy to make. And since they're made from scraps of fabric, snippets of paper, and small pieces of ribbon and lace, they're also inexpensive, allowing more room for profits.

While browsing, you may notice a few detailed pieces that don't appear to be quick and easy at all. These ambitious designs are offered for raffle prizes or special-order projects.

But before beginning to cut and stitch, be sure to read over Supplies and Techniques, beginning on page 154. In that chapter, I share some hints that will help you make beautiful, fine-quality handmades.

Now get comfortable, pour yourself a cup of tea, and turn the page for dozens of ideas for making your next fund-raiser a fun-raiser—a Four Star Bazaar!

GIFTS GALORE

Y ou're starting in the **right** place! These fabric and paper projects won't take much time, and they're really quite **easy** to make. This chapter is filled with **lots** of little gifts—sachets, pin-cushions, pot holders, note cards, and more. Ready, get set,

sew!

BANDANNA BONANZA

The pretty corners of one wide-bordered bandanna provide enough material to make four heart pot holders. The hemmed scraps that remain can be stitched into petite sachets to tuck among kitchen linens. And bandanna motifs can be embroidered on Felt Bunny Magnets to coordinate with the pot holders. To make the Bandanna Basket, follow instructions for the Soft Basket on page 36, using bandanna border sections for the basket and a coordinating fabric for the lining.

Bandanna Heart Pot Holders

Materials for one pot holder
Pattern on page 27
10″ square corner of bandanna with 4″-wide border
10″ square of black fabric for backing
Thread to match
10″ square of extra-thick quilt batting
1⅛ yards (½″-wide) of black double-fold bias tape
Vanishing fabric marker

Instructions
1. Trace pattern on folded paper and cut out.
2. Centering tip of heart pattern on bandanna corner, pin pattern to fabric. With marker, trace around shape. *Do not cut out yet.*
3. Stack backing fabric, right side down; batting; and bandanna, right side up. Pin and baste layers together. Machine-stitch along outline. Cut out heart, adding ⅜″ seam allowance.
4. Cut 6½″ of bias tape and reserve for hanger. Bind edges of heart with remaining bias tape, mitering tape at heart center top and tip. To make hanger, turn under and stitch cut ends of reserved tape. Fold tape to form loop and tack it to back of heart at center top.

Felt Bunny Pin or Magnet

Materials for one bunny
Pattern on page 27
3″ x 6″ scrap of felt
Embroidery floss: black, white
Polyester stuffing
White glue
Magnetic tape (for magnet) or safety pin (for pin)
3½″ (⅛″-wide) of black ribbon
Vanishing fabric marker

Instructions
1. Trace pattern and cut out.
2. Cut felt in half to make 2 (3″) squares. For front, use marker to trace bunny and markings onto 1 square. For back, trace bunny onto other square, omitting markings. Cut out shape on outline. Cut 1″ slit in center of bunny back.
3. With 1 strand of black embroidery floss, satin-stitch eye. With 2 strands of floss, embroider flower with lazy daisy stitches and French knots as shown in photograph.
4. With wrong sides facing, join front and back with blanket stitches all around bunny, using 2 strands of black floss. Stuff slightly. Slipstitch opening closed. Glue strip of magnetic tape (for magnet) or tack safety pin (for pin) to back of bunny. Tie ribbon in bow and tack to bunny's neck.

Bright bandannas are used to make these easy projects: heart-shaped pot holders, matching Felt Bunny Magnets, and a Soft Basket full of lavender sachet bags.

Bandanna
Sachet Bag

Materials for one bag

Scraps from hemmed border of
   bandanna
Thread to match
7″ of black medium rickrack
Polyester stuffing
Dried lavender
⅓ yard (¼″-wide) of black
   grosgrain ribbon

Instructions

1. Cut 2 (3¾″ x 5⅝″) rectangles from
bandanna border, with 1 (3¾″) end of
each rectangle at hemmed edge of
bandanna.
2. With right sides of rectangles facing, machine-stitch ¼″ from edge
around 3 sides, leaving hemmed edge
open. Clip lower corners and turn bag.
Stitch rickrack trim around top edge.
3. Place a small amount of lavender in
stuffing and stuff bag to within 1½″ of
top. Tie ribbon in a bow around bag
top. If desired, tack top edges together
at seams to conceal allowances.

STAR BRIGHT BASICS

With star patterns borrowed from other projects in this book, you can quickly produce this galaxy of stellar sellers.

Treat your bazaar customers to a shower of stars, from the Starbaby Tooth Pillow to a trio of star-bright shirts.

TIP

Your customers are sure to appreciate a gift-wrap service. Use donated papers, ribbons, and bows, and charge a small fee.

Starbaby Tooth Pillow

Materials

Pattern on page 28
4¾" x 13" piece of yellow fabric
2¾" x 5½" piece of yellow print fabric
Thread to match
Embroidery floss: dark pink, medium blue
Polyester stuffing
Vanishing fabric marker
Powder blush
Cotton swab

Instructions

1. Trace pattern, transferring markings. Cut out.

2. On wrong side of yellow fabric, use marker to trace 2 Starbaby shapes and 1 pocket ½" apart. Transfer face and topstitching markings to right side of 1 fabric star. Transfer pocket placement line and slit to right side of second fabric star. Cut out all pieces, adding ¼" seam allowance.

3. Embroider Starbaby face, using 2 strands of pink floss to backstitch mouth and 1 strand of blue floss to satin-stitch eyes.

4. To make Starbaby, cut slit as indicated on back. With right sides facing and raw edges aligned, stitch completely around star. Trim seam and clip curves and angles. Turn star right side out through slit. Stuff star to make it firm, but flat, and slipstitch slit closed.

5. With right sides facing, fold pocket in half along fold line and stitch around curved edge, leaving small opening for turning. Turn. Slipstitch opening closed.

Pin pocket on back of Starbaby at placement line, covering slit. By hand, stitch curved edge to star. By hand, topstitch circle around face, where indicated, through all layers.

6. To make Startoy, on wrong side of print fabric, trace Startoy shape. Transfer markings to right side of fabric and embroider as for Starbaby face, using 1 strand of floss for all embroidery. Cut out, adding ¼" seam allowances.

Cut 2 (1⅝" x 2¾") pieces of print fabric. With right sides facing and raw edges aligned, run ¼" seam down 1 long side, leaving ¾" opening at center of seam. Press seam open.

With right sides facing, stitch Startoy front to seamed back piece. Trim seam and clip curves and angles. Turn and stuff. Slipstitch opening closed. Topstitch around face through all layers as indicated on pattern.

With cotton swab, lightly dab cheeks of both Starbaby and Startoy with blush. Tack Startoy to Starbaby (see photograph).

**Star Bright Basic shirts suit the entire family.
From left, Shooting Star Toddler's Shirt, All Star T-Shirt, and Starlight Sweatshirt.**

Starlight Sweatshirt

Materials
**Star Lollipop pattern on page 152
Child's sweatshirt
6 (3½″) squares of fabric in 6
    different rainbow colors
6 (3″) squares of paper-backed
    fusible web
7½″ x 12″ piece of tear-away
    interfacing
Thread to match**

Instructions
Note: Wash and dry sweatshirt, following label directions.

1. Trace and cut out pattern. Transfer pattern to paper side of each piece of web. *Do not cut out shapes yet.* Following manufacturer's instructions, fuse 1 square of web to wrong side of each fabric square. Cut out stars without adding seam allowance. Peel off paper backing.

2. Arrange stars on front of sweatshirt as in photograph. The side points of each star should touch.

3. Fuse each appliqué to shirt. On inside of shirt front, baste tear-away interfacing behind appliqués. Zigzag-stitch around edges of each star, using matching thread. Remove basting and tear away interfacing.

This starry assortment of decorative shirts will draw shoppers both old and young. From left, Shooting Star Toddler's Shirt, All Star T-Shirt, and Starlight Sweatshirt.

Shooting Star Toddler's Shirt

Materials

Star Lollipop pattern on page 152
Toddler's sweatshirt
3½″ square of bright yellow fabric
Thread to match
3½″ x 20″ piece of paper-backed fusible web
13″ (1½″-wide) of rainbow ribbon
3½″ x 15″ piece of tear-away interfacing
Black embroidery floss

Instructions

Note: Wash and dry sweatshirt, following label directions.

1. Trace and cut out pattern. Follow Step 1 of Starlight Sweatshirt, page 13.

2. Cut piece of fusible web length and width of ribbon. Following manufacturer's instructions, fuse web to wrong side of ribbon. Peel off paper backing. With front of shirt facing you, open lower left side seam from top of waistband to 1¾″ above waistband. Position ribbon and star on shirt as shown in photograph and fuse to shirt.

3. Baste tear-away interfacing inside shirt front behind ribbon and star. With matching thread, topstitch edges of ribbon to shirt. Zigzag-stitch along

edge of star. Tear away interfacing and close side seam. Transfer eyes and mouth from Diagram to star. With 1 strand of embroidery floss, satin-stitch eyes and backstitch mouth.

Diagram: Shooting Star Facial Features

All Star T-shirt

Materials
Heart Star Ornament pattern on page 144
Adult T-shirt
12 (5½″) squares of fabric in 12 different rainbow colors
12 (5½″) squares of paper-backed fusible web
3 (5½″ x 20″) pieces of tear-away interfacing
Thread to match
White pencil

Instructions
Note: Wash and dry T-shirt, following label directions.
1. Trace and cut out pattern, omitting heart at center. Follow step 1 of Starlight Sweatshirt, page 13.
2. With pencil, mark 3 horizontal lines across front of shirt, placing first line 4¼″ above bottom edge of shirt; second line 10¼″ above bottom of shirt; and third line 15¼″ above bottom of shirt. On front of shirt, center 4 stars on top line, with top horizontal edges on pencil line and side star points touching.
3. Follow Step 3 of Starlight Sweatshirt for fusing, stitching, and interfacing. Add remaining rows of stars.

ICE CREAM SHOP

Dripping ice cream appliqués embellish the front of this fun-to-wear "sweetshirt." To make the drips, sort out the ice cream colors from a bag of multicolored pom-poms. Match them to your yummiest fabric scraps, which make the ice cream scoops.

Use the simple ice cream motif to make other great gifts: a soft baby rattle and a cute pincushion. Scoop up the leftover scraps to make quick pins and kitchen magnets.

Sherbet-colored fabric scraps form the ice cream scoops on this "sweetshirt."

Ice Cream Sweetshirt

Materials
Pattern on page 29
White sweatshirt
6" x 7" scrap of tan fabric
3 (5") squares of fabric in ice cream colors
6" x 7" scrap of paper-backed fusible web
Thread to match
½" acrylic pom-poms to match fabrics
Vanishing fabric marker

Instructions
Note: Wash and dry sweatshirt, following label directions.

1. Trace pattern, transferring markings. Cut out.

2. Trace 3 cones on paper side of fusible web. Following manufacturer's instructions, fuse web to wrong side of tan fabric. Cut out cones along outlines. Peel off paper backing.

3. With wrong sides facing, fold each fabric square on bias to form triangle. Using pattern, cut 1 scoop from each fabric. Leaving scoop folded, make a

row of gathering stitches along seam line. Gather semicircle tightly until gathered edge measures 2". Fasten off. Baste bottom of scoop to top of cone, having scoop's seam allowance behind cone. Repeat with other 2 scoops and cones.

4. Using marker, draw center line down front of shirt. Center and pin 1

cone on this line. Pin remaining cones 1½" from center cone (see photograph). Fuse to shirt front. Machine-satin-stitch around top and side edges of cones. Make second horizontal row of satin stitches ⅜" below first row on top edge of each cone.

5. Randomly tack poms-poms to shirt below each cone (see photograph).

16

Ice Cream Rattle or Pincushion

Materials for one cone
Pattern on pages 29-30
7½" square of tan fabric
7½" square of flannel
6" square of pink or green fabric
Thread to match
Embroidery floss for rattle: dark brown, pink
Polyester stuffing
Large jingle bell for rattle
Vanishing fabric marker

Instructions
1. Trace pattern, transferring markings. Cut out.

2. With edges aligned and wrong sides facing, baste tan fabric to flannel. Machine-quilt ½" grid through both layers. With marker, trace cone on tan fabric and scoop on pink or green fabric. Transfer pattern markings to fabric and cut out both pieces.

3. Fold cone with right sides facing and raw edges aligned. Stitch long straight edge of cone, leaving open between Xs. Trim seam to ⅛", except at opening. Clip tip. *Do not turn yet.*

4. If making rattle, embroider face on scoop. With 1 strand of brown floss, satin-stitch eyes and backstitch mouth. With 2 strands of pink, satin-stitch cheeks. Run row of gathering stitches along seam line. Pull threads to gather slightly.

5. With right sides facing and raw edges aligned, lay scoop inside top of cone. Pull basting thread to gather scoop to fit top of cone. Baste edges of scoop and cone together. Machine-stitch. Trim seam and clip curves. Turn cone and scoop right side out through opening. Stuff firmly. If making rattle, bury jingle bell deeply in stuffing. Slip-stitch opening closed. Add second line of slipstitches for extra safety if making rattle.

Ice Cream Pin or Magnet

Materials for fifteen cones
Pattern on page 30
6" x 8½" scrap of tan felt
15 (3") squares of colored fabric or 15 colored 1" pom-poms
Tan thread
Polyester stuffing
White glue
15 tiny safety pins (for pins)
Adhesive-backed magnetic tape (for magnets)
Vanishing fabric marker
Toothpick

Instructions
1. Trace pattern and cut out. (If using pom-poms for scoops, omit scoop pattern piece.)

2. With ¹⁄₁₆"-wide zigzag-stitches, stitch ¼" grid pattern on felt. Place cone pattern on felt as shown in Diagram. With marker, trace cone on felt. Remove pattern and machine-satin-stitch along entire outline. Trim cone close to stitched outline. Curl cone around finger. Butt straight edges together and join with slipstitches. Stuff cone.

3. (If using pom-poms, omit this step.) Transfer scoop pattern to colored fabric and cut out. With doubled thread, make row of gathering stitches ¼" from cut edge. Pull thread to gather slightly. Insert small amount of stuffing inside scoop. Pull thread, adding more stuffing to make scoop firm. Pull thread tight, wrap around bottom of scoop, and tie off.

4. With toothpick, spread thin line of glue around inside rim of cone. Place fabric scoop or pom-pom inside cone. Let dry. Sew tiny pin to cone at seam or add narrow strip of magnetic tape. Repeat for 14 more pins or magnets.

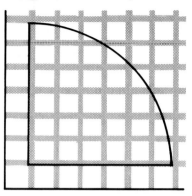

Diagram: Pattern placement

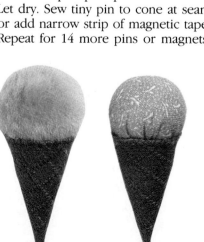

SMALL WHIMSIES

Gather your friends together and create a boothful of these tiny treasures in just one busy afternoon. Cultivate a whole colony of Mushroom Pincushions, using bargain spools of thread and small scraps of soft cotton fabrics. A bit of dried lavender makes the Sachet Parasol a fragrant gift item. And let your imagination go wild to create your own Magnet Merriment.

Magnet Merriment

Materials
Garment labels
Ribbon scraps in widths to match garment labels
Polyester stuffing (for garment label magnets)
Spools of thread
Buttons
½" magnets or self-sticking magnetic tape
White glue (if using ½" magnets)

Instructions
1. For garment label magnet, cut piece of ribbon ½" longer than garment label. Press under ¼" on each cut end. With wrong sides facing and edges aligned, slipstitch label to ribbon across top, bottom, and 1 end. Stuff, and slipstitch open end closed. Glue magnet to back, or cut small piece of magnetic tape and attach to back.
2. For spool and button magnets, glue magnets or attach small pieces of magnetic tape to backs of items.

The materials list for this project is really endless. It can also include seashells, pennies, crayons, bells, clothespins—just about anything you can round up and attach to a magnet.

For other interesting magnets, look for old jewelry, antique buttons, quaint keys, or even party favors and dollhouse accessories.

Sachet Parasol

Materials for one parasol
Pattern on page 31
6" x 9" scrap of miniprint fabric
Thread to match
11" (¼"-wide) of gathered lace
12" of chenille stem
Dried lavender flowers
12" (⅛"-wide) of satin ribbon

Instructions
1. Trace pattern, transferring markings. Cut out.
2. From miniprint, cut 1 parasol. Press under ¼" seam allowance along curved edge of parasol piece. With narrow stitch, zigzag-stitch bound edge of lace along pressed-under seam allowance. Trim seam allowance close to stitching. Fold with right sides facing and straight edges aligned. Machine-stitch from dot to lace edge. Press seam open. *Do not turn.*
3. Fold 4" of 1 end of chenille stem down and twist it around itself in spiral fashion. Curve twisted tip into hook (see Diagram). Fold down ¾" of opposite end of stem but do not twist. Slide ½" of this end through small opening in parasol. Handstitch ⅛" from edge to secure parasol to stem. Turn parasol right side out.
4. With doubled thread, run row of gathering stitches along gathering line on parasol. Pour 2 tablespoons of lavender flowers into the parasol. Pull threads to gather around chenille stem and knot. Wrap the ribbon around gathering thread and tie in bow.

Diagram: Making parasol

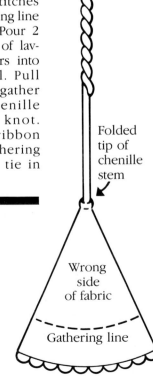

Folded tip of chenille stem

Wrong side of fabric

Gathering line

Mushroom Pincushions

Materials for one pincushion
Pattern on page 31
6" x 9" scrap of cotton fabric
Thread to match
3" Styrofoam ball
Heavy-duty thread or dental floss
Large spool of thread
White glue
Assorted pins and needles
Vanishing fabric marker

Instructions
1. Trace pattern and cut out.
2. Using marker, draw line around exact center of Styrofoam ball. Wrap piece of heavy-duty thread around line you've drawn. Cross and pull ends of thread tight, cutting ball in half. Roll cut edge of 1 half against smooth, firm surface to round off edges. Reserve other half of ball to make another mushroom.
3. Place pattern pieces ½" apart on single layer of fabric and trace around them with marker. Cut out each piece, adding ¼" seam allowances.

Using doubled thread, run row of very small handstitches along seam line of cap top. Leaving 5" tails at beginning and end, cut needle free. Pull thread ends to gather circle slightly. Place Styrofoam cap inside fabric circle and pull threads tightly to gather fabric snugly around cap. Adjust gathers evenly. Fasten off.

On cap base, clip curves, finger-press seam allowance under, and baste. Center base on bottom of cap top, covering gathering stitches. Pin and whipstitch fabrics together.
4. Locate thread end on spool. On opposite end of spool, spread layer of glue. Center mushroom cap on spool and press to adhere. Allow to dry. Insert a few pins and needles in cap.

Magnets made from buttons, small spools of thread, and garment labels surround two pretty Sachet Parasols. Below them are three handy Mushroom Pincushions.

19

Much of the work involved in making these paper projects is done for you. A big box of white envelopes provides perfect companions for the Animal Note Cards. The portfolios are made from purchased folders. And decorative stickers can be bought, several sheets to a packet, in a variety of shapes.

SIMPLE PROJECTS FROM PAPER

Even those who aren't handy with needle and thread will find the following projects easy to complete—there's no sewing required.

The whimsical Animal Note Cards are cut from fabric-covered art paper and tucked into standard envelopes. To make the portfolios in the photograph, cut the animal shapes from self-adhesive decorative paper and use them to embellish purchased folders. Add a few stickers and ribbons and you're done.

Animal Note Cards

Materials for one note card
Patterns on page 32
Scrap of sturdy paper (4″ x 13″ for pig, 6¼″ x 7½″ for kitten)
Same-size scrap of fabric
Same-size scrap of paper-backed fusible web
White envelope (3⅝″ x 6½″)
Paper clips
Craft knife
Paper punches (⅛″ for eyes; ¼″ for pig's tail)

Instructions
1. Trace pattern, transferring markings. Cut out.
2. Place web, paper side up, on wrong side of fabric scrap. Following manufacturer's instructions, fuse web to fabric. Peel off paper backing.

Fuse web to card. Score on paper side and fold in half, fabric side out, to measure 4″ x 6½″ for pig and 3¾″ x 6¼″ for kitten.
3. Aligning fold line with fold on card, place pattern on card and hold in place with paper clips. Trace. Remove pattern but leave clips in place. On protected surface, cut out animal shape with craft knife. Punch out eyes and pig's tail through all layers.

PAPER CORNER BOOKMARKS

These paper bookmarks are designed to hug the corner of a page. They make nice additions to book gifts, and the simple shapes can double as gift tags. Just omit the glue tabs.

Bookmarks

Materials for one bookmark
Patterns on page 33
3" x 5" scrap of sturdy colored paper
Red paper for bird's heart and bear's cheeks
Black paper for bear's nose and eyes
White glue
Paper clips
Craft knife
Paper punches (⅛" for eyes; ¼" for bear's cheeks and nose)
Black fine-point marker

Instructions

1. Trace pattern, transferring markings. Cut out.
2. Score and fold paper scrap in half to form 2½" x 3" rectangle. For bird, heart, or bunny, place fold line on pattern on folded edge of paper and hold in place with paper clips. Trace shape and remove pattern. Leave clips in place. With craft knife, cut out shape, except on fold. (Bear has no fold line. Cut 2 separate bear pieces.)
3. Open bookmark and score fold line on 1 tab. Cut off tab on opposite side (except for bunny tail). Glue tab to inside of opposite side of bookmark. (For bear, use 2 ears as tabs. For bunny, use 1 tail as tab.) From red paper, cut tiny heart for bird. Using paper punches, punch 1 (¼") circle from black paper for bear's nose; punch 2 (¼") circles from red paper for bear's cheeks; punch 2 (⅛") circles from black paper for bear's eyes. Glue in place. With black marker, draw eyes on bird and bunny and mouth on bear (see photograph).

A MOUSE FOR ALL SEASONS

Stitched in springtime pastels, summer's brilliant palette, or autumn's muted hues, this adaptable creature can become a pincushion, a sachet, or a child's pocket toy. When winter comes, use Christmas prints and make mousekins to hide among the tree branches, scamper over packages, or snuggle into the top of a stocking.

Mouse

Materials for one mouse
Pattern on page 33
4¼" x 12" scrap of print fabric
Thread to match
Black embroidery floss
6" (1⁄16"-wide) of coordinating
   satin ribbon
Polyester stuffing
Vanishing fabric marker

Instructions
1. Trace pattern, transferring markings. Cut out.
2. For mouse base, cut 2 (2" x 4¼") pieces from fabric. With right sides facing, stitch ¼" seam along 1 long side, leaving 1" opening in center of seam. Press seam open and set aside.

For ears, cut 2 (1¾" x 4¼") pieces from fabric and pin together, right sides facing. With marker, trace 2 ears ¼" from edge of fabric and ½" apart. *Do not cut out ears yet.* Stitch around curved edge of each ear on outline, leaving straight edges open. Cut out

ears, adding ¼" seam allowances. Clip curves and turn ears right side out. Set aside.

On wrong side of remaining fabric, trace 1 head and 1 body, ½" apart, transferring markings. With 1 strand of embroidery floss, satin-stitch eyes. Cut out head and body, adding ¼" seam allowances.
3. Run row of small gathering stitches ¼" from straight edge of each ear. Pull thread to gather each ear to ⅞". Knot thread.

With raw edges aligned, baste ears between dots on straight edge of mouse body on right side of fabric. With right sides facing and ears between, baste head to body along straight edge. Machine-stitch. Press seam toward head. Fold ears toward center of mouse and tack in place to avoid catching them in side seams. For tail, fold ribbon in half. With raw edges aligned and loop pointing toward head, stitch ribbon ends to right side of body at tail dot.

With right sides facing, center mouse top on previously prepared mouse base. With ¼" seam, machine-stitch around entire mouse. Trim seam and clip curves. Turn mouse through opening in base. Remove tack stitches from ears. Stuff body firmly and slip-stitch opening closed.

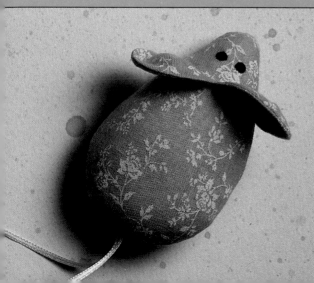

MAMA CAT AND KITTEN MESSAGE BOARD

Enlarge the kitten note card pattern to make this prize-winning message board. Use the pattern actual size to make a kitten pocket to hold a note pad or index cards. Make the cat and kitten from two similarly colored compatible prints and a slightly darker sewing thread. Add a matching colored pencil to complete a raffle prize that your bazaar patrons will love.

Message Board

Materials
Kitten Note pattern on page 32
9″ x 14½″ piece of print fabric for board
4¼″ x 6¼″ piece of coordinating print fabric for pocket
8″ x 12½″ (¼″-thick) piece of foam core board
8″ x 12½″ piece of drawing paper (coordinating with fabric)
9″ x 14½″ piece of thin polyester quilt batting
4⅛″ x 6⅛″ piece of heavy fusible interfacing
White glue
Liquid ravel preventer (optional)
Masking tape
Sewing thread slightly darker than fabric
1″ x 2″ scrap of colored paper
15″ (¼″-wide) of ribbon
24″ (⅜″-wide) of ribbon
Short colored pencil
3″ x 5″ note pad or index cards
Self-adhesive foam tape
Straight pins with plastic heads
Craft knife
Vanishing fabric marker
Paper punch (⅛″ diameter)

Instructions
1. For pocket, trace and cut out Kitten Note pattern. To enlarge kitten pattern for board, draw 1″ grid on 8″ x 13″ piece of paper and follow instructions for enlarging patterns in Supplies and Techniques.

2. Trace enlarged pattern on foam core and use craft knife to cut out. For backing, trace enlarged cat pattern on drawing paper and cut out ¹⁄₁₆″ inside outline. Trace cat on batting. Cut out, adding ½″ all around. Trace cat on large fabric piece and cut out, adding 1″ all around.

3. Clip almost to outline around batting cat shape, making cuts ½″ apart. Also clip sharp angles at ears and neck. Cut a few notches from batting around ears so that it will wrap around board smoothly. Center and glue batting to foam core, wrapping edges of batting to back of foam core. Let dry.

Clip curves of cat fabric shape. If desired for greater stability, apply liquid ravel preventer to angles at ears and neck. Allow to dry and clip these areas. Center batting side of cat board on wrong side of fabric. Alternating from top to bottom and side to side, pull fabric to back of board and tape with masking tape, keeping tape ⅛″ from edge of board. Glue backing paper to back of board, covering fabric edges. Place board under several books and let dry.

4. Following manufacturer's instructions, fuse interfacing to wrong side of pocket fabric. Trace kitten pattern on right side of fabric. Mark eye placement with marker. With ¹⁄₁₆″-wide stitches, zigzag-stitch along kitten outline. Cut out, being careful not to cut stitches.

5. From colored paper, punch out eyes for kitten and cut out 2 (¼″) circles for cat eyes. Glue in place. Tie narrow ribbon in bow around kitten's neck. Tie wider ribbon in bow around cat's neck. Pin kitten pocket in place on cat board (see photograph). Slip-stitch kitten to cat along sides and bottom of kitten. Tuck colored pencil and note pad in pocket.

To hang board on wall, attach small piece of foam tape near top of board and 1 near bottom, leaving outside cover paper on tape until ready to hang. Stick a few pins in front of message board to hold notes.

Placed above the telephone or in the kitchen, this message board is a great place to tack notes, grocery lists, and frequently called phone numbers.

TIPS

The charity bazaar is as American as a Fourth of July parade.

In days gone by, bazaars were rural events held to raise money for the church or for a political or charity cause. Sale items were handmade donations—quilts, aprons, bonnets, toys, home-baked items, and canned goods.

Today, bazaars are held in the city as well as in the country—in shopping malls, school yards, civic centers, and even in private homes. But as in the old days, the best bazaars still offer handmade treasures.

And it's as true today as it was back then: The most successful bazaars are well planned and organized. Of course, each bazaar is different, but they also share some common goals and problems. Here are a few fundamental rules to get you headed toward a Four-Star Bazaar!

Call a planning meeting. This should take place as far ahead of the bazaar date as possible. A year is ideal.

Elect a general chairperson as well as committee chairpersons for booths, publicity, concessions, entertainment, etc.

Make a list of craftspeople who might be willing to donate items. Include potential "happy hands" who might make craft items for a small fee or a percentage of sales. Write letters to potential crafters, and follow up with phone calls. Give examples of the kinds of crafts you need but be open for suggestions from craft volunteers.

Choose a theme. This isn't a must for a successful bazaar, but it can give your fair a unified appearance and help simplify decorating. Old-fashioned, nostalgic themes are particularly popular. Outfit your bazaar as a "Country Store," or plan the event around a "County Fair" theme, with games and refreshments as well as sale items.

Bandanna Heart
Pot Holders

Instructions are on page 10.

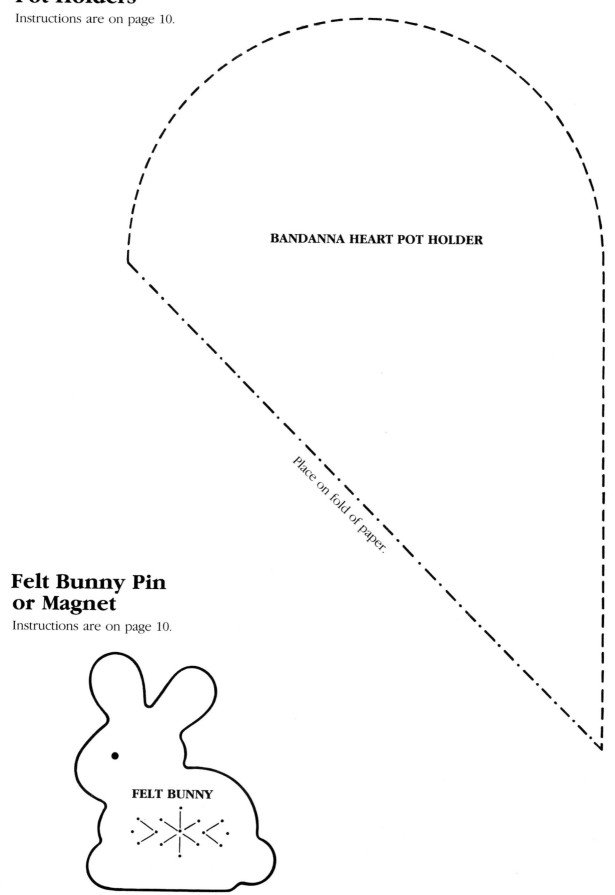

BANDANNA HEART POT HOLDER

Place on fold of paper.

Felt Bunny Pin
or Magnet

Instructions are on page 10.

FELT BUNNY

Starbaby Tooth Pillow

Instructions are on page 12.

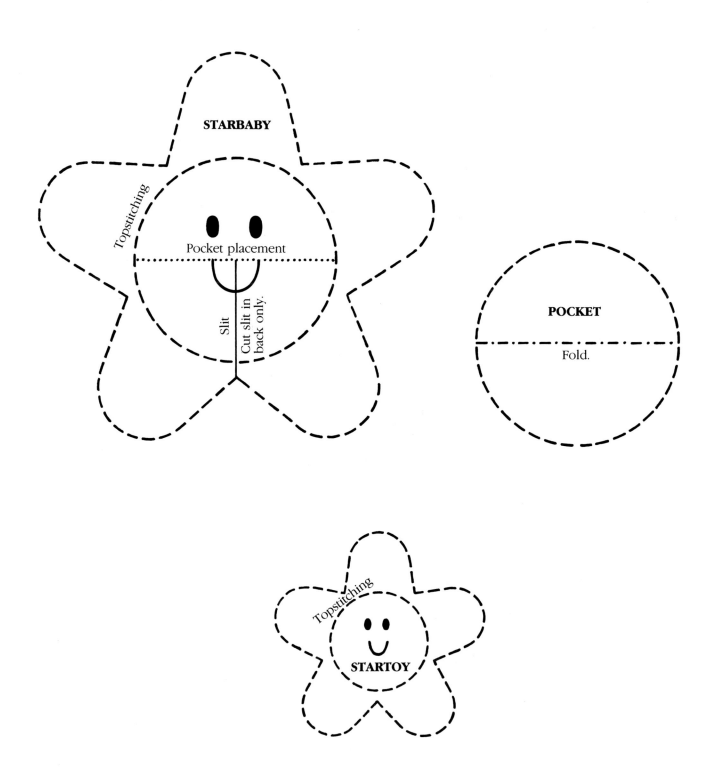

STARBABY

Topstitching

Pocket placement

Slit

Cut slit in back only.

POCKET

Fold.

Topstitching

STARTOY

Ice Cream
Sweetshirt

Instructions are on page 16.

Place on bias fold of fabric.

SWEETSHIRT SCOOP

SWEETSHIRT CONE

Ice Cream Rattle
or Pincushion

Instructions are on page 17.

Place on fold of paper.

ICE CREAM SCOOP

(RATTLE OR PINCUSHION)

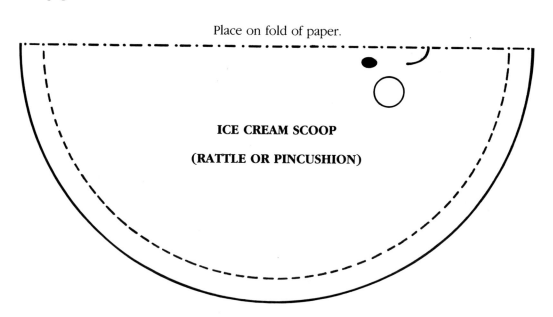

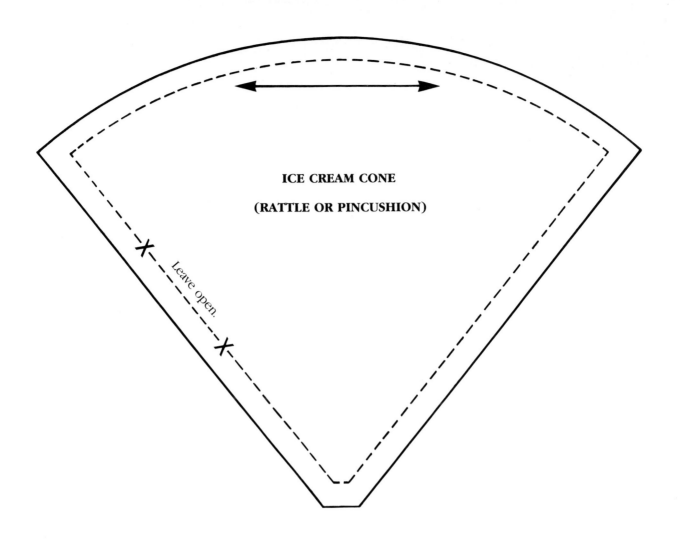

ICE CREAM CONE

(RATTLE OR PINCUSHION)

Leave open.

Ice Cream Pin
or Magnet

Instructions are on page 17.

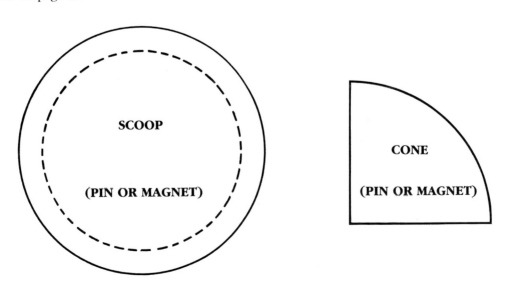

SCOOP

(PIN OR MAGNET)

CONE

(PIN OR MAGNET)

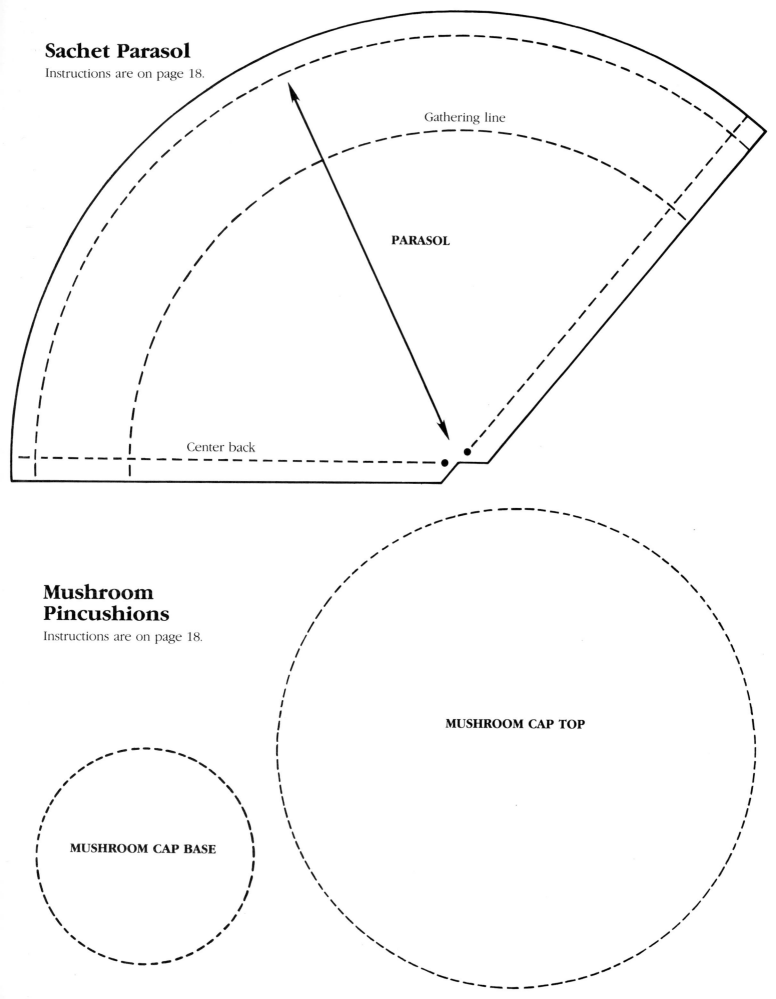

Sachet Parasol

Instructions are on page 18.

Gathering line

PARASOL

Center back

Mushroom Pincushions

Instructions are on page 18.

MUSHROOM CAP TOP

MUSHROOM CAP BASE

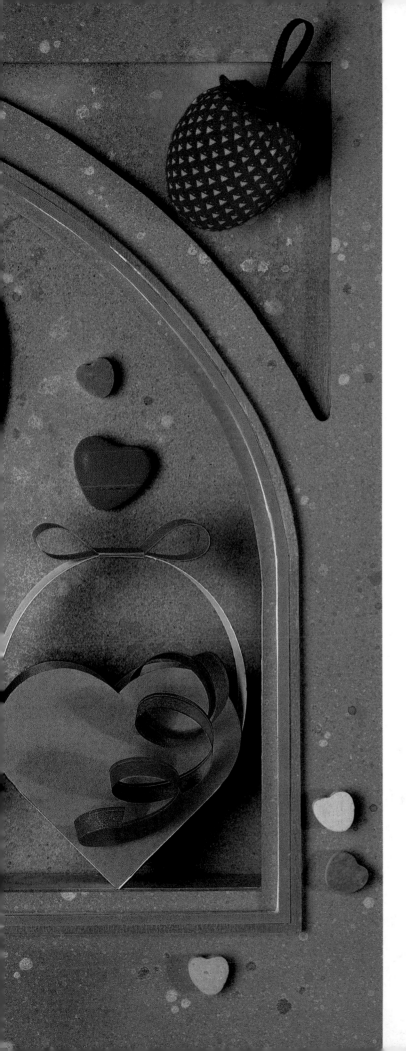

HOLIDAY FAIR

Here's a cache of **ideas** for every season and every reason—baskets **full** of bunnies and eggs, Halloween **treats** for young and old, romantic valentines, patriotic flags! Make these seasonal items to sell at special events, or create them for your family's **enjoyment.**

EASTER PARADE

Bring together all your pretty pastel scraps to make an Easter basket filled with Funny Bunnies and Calico Eggs. Fill Paper Bunny Baskets with jelly beans for springtime party favors. Trim a Fuzzy Bunny Bib with bright colors to make Easter more fun for a little one.

Calico Eggs

Materials for one egg
Pattern on page 58
2 (4½") squares of print fabric
Thread to match
Polyester stuffing
Vanishing fabric marker

Instructions
1. Trace pattern, transferring markings. Cut out.
2. With right sides facing, baste fabric squares together. With marker, trace 2 egg shapes on layered fabric. *Do not cut out yet.*
3. Machine-stitch center seam of each shape. Cut out each shape, adding ⅛" seam allowance. Clip curves. Open out each egg unit. With right sides facing and seams aligned at top and bottom, pin units together. Machine-stitch around egg, leaving 1 side open between Xs. Trim seam and clip curves except at opening. Turn.
4. Stuff egg and slipstitch opening closed. Roll egg between hands, molding it into egg shape.

Funny Bunnies

Materials for one bunny
Pattern on page 58
2 (4½" x 8") scraps of print fabric
Thread to match
Polyester stuffing
½" white pom-pom
Black embroidery floss
12" (1⁄16"-wide) of satin ribbon
Vanishing fabric marker

Instructions
1. Trace pattern, transferring markings. Cut out.
2. With right sides facing, pin fabric scraps together. Lay pattern pieces on fabric ½" apart and, with marker, trace 2 body sections, 2 paws, 2 ears, and 1 piece for feet. *Do not cut out shapes.*
3. Machine-stitch center seam of body front. Machine-stitch center seam of body back, leaving seam open between Xs. Stitch around remaining shapes, leaving open as indicated. Cut out shapes, adding ⅛" seam allowances. Clip curves, except at openings, and turn pieces. Open body units and finger-press seams open.
4. Press ears. Fold ears as indicated and tack (see photograph). On body front, with right sides facing, raw edges aligned, and ears pointing toward bottom of body, baste ears on each side of center seam. Stuff paws lightly and stitch openings closed. With right sides facing and paws pointing toward tummy, baste paws in place on body front between dots. Stuff feet lightly. Slipstitch opening closed. Topstitch down center of feet as indicated.
5. With right sides facing and seams aligned at top and bottom, pin bunny front and back together. Machine-stitch around body. Be careful not to catch free ends of ears or paws in seam. Trim seam and clip curves. Turn bunny through opening.
Stuff body firmly. Slipstitch opening closed. Roll body between hands, molding it into egg shape. Slipstitch feet to bottom of body, matching feet topstitching with center body seam. Tack pom-pom to bunny for tail.
6. With 2 strands of floss, embroider French knots for eyes. With 1 strand of floss, embroider bunny's mouth (see photograph).
Wrap ribbon around bunny just above paws and tie bow at center front. Tack ribbon at sides of bunny.

Soft Basket

Materials
Pattern on pages 58-59
10" x 22" piece of fabric for basket
10" x 22" piece of muslin for lining
10" x 22" piece of quilt batting
Thread to match
2 yards (¼"-wide) of double-fold bias tape

Instructions
1. On folded paper, trace basket side and basket handle pieces. Trace basket base on flat paper. Transfer markings and cut out.
2. From basket fabric, cut 1 base, 1 side, and 1 handle, adding ¼" seam allowances. Repeat for lining and batting pieces.
3. Baste batting to wrong side of basket side. With right sides facing, stitch ends of basket side piece. Trim batting close to stitching line and press seam open. Turn right side out.
With right sides facing, stitch ends of lining side piece together. Press seam open. Place lining side piece inside basket side piece, matching seams, with wrong sides facing and batting between. Machine-stitch ¼" from each edge. Along 1 edge, clip seam allowance at ¼" intervals.
4. Stack base, right side down; batting base; and lining base. Machine-stitch on seam line through all layers.
5. With lining sides facing, pin clipped edge of basket side to base, centering seam on 1 side. (Seam allowances will be outside basket.) Machine-stitch on seam line.
6. Trim seam allowance to ⅛" around base and top of basket. Bind edges with bias tape.
7. Stack handle pieces as for base. Machine-stitch layers along all sides on seam line. Trim seam allowance to ⅛". Bind edges of handle with bias tape, mitering corners. Slipstitch handle to inside of basket (see photograph).

Celebrate Easter and the coming of spring with these easy-to-stitch projects: a fabric basket full of Calico Eggs and Funny Bunnies and a plush bunny bib adorned with carrot ties.

Fuzzy Bunny Bib

Materials

Pattern on page 60
9″ x 11″ piece of white terry
  velour fabric
9″ x 14″ piece of bright pink
  miniprint fabric
5″ x 7″ piece of orange fabric
9″ x 12″ piece of thin quilt
  batting
Thread to match
Embroidery floss: pink, black
2⅔ yards (¼″-wide) of green
  double-fold bias tape
Polyester stuffing
Vanishing fabric marker

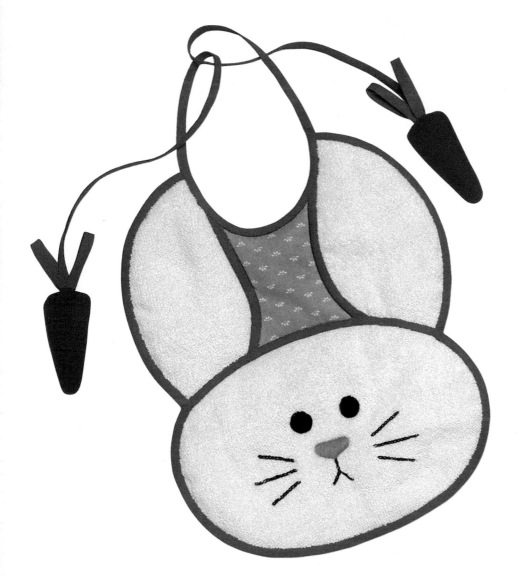

Instructions

1. On folded paper, trace bunny bib pattern piece. On flat paper, trace remaining pattern pieces. Transfer all markings. Cut out pattern pieces.

2. Cut 1 bunny bib from white terry velour, 1 from pink miniprint, and 1 from batting. Cut 1 background piece from pink miniprint.

Cut orange fabric in half to make 2 (3½″ x 5″) pieces. Baste right sides together. With marker, trace 2 carrot shapes on fabric. Transfer markings. *Do not cut out carrots yet.*

On right side of white velour face, use 2 strands of floss to satin-stitch pink nose and black eyes and chain-stitch black mouth and whiskers.

3. Stack backing, right side down; batting; and bunny front, right side up. Baste layers together. Machine-stitch on all bias tape placement lines on bib.

4. Cut 2 (4½″) lengths and 1 (7¼″) length of bias tape. Open center fold of each piece and trim away ⅛″ along 1 edge to reduce bulk.

Pin pink background piece in place between ears, matching dots on background piece with dots at top and bottom of ears. Slipstitch 4½″ pieces of bias tape in place over dotted lines on inside edges of ears, covering edges of pink background. Stitch 7¼″ piece of tape to head top along dotted lines between Xs, covering lower edge of pink fabric.

Cut 31″ length of bias tape and bind outside edge of bib, leaving bib neck between tips of ears unbound.

Cut 30″ length of tape and bind bib neck, leaving 12″ tie on each end. Stitch edges of ties closed.

5. Machine-stitch carrots on outline, leaving openings as indicated. Cut out each carrot, leaving ⅛″ seam allowance. Clip curves. Turn carrots right side out and stuff.

To make carrots' leaves, cut 4 (3½″) lengths of bias tape and stitch edges closed. Fold 2 lengths of tape in half to form loops. Tuck ends of loops and end of 1 tie into 1 open carrot top and slipstitch opening closed. Repeat with other carrot and tie.

Pastel Paper Bunny Baskets make whimsical containers for Easter candy.

Paper Bunny Basket

Materials for one basket
Pattern on page 61
9¾″ square of colored art paper
1¼ yards (⅛″-wide) of ribbon
⅛″ paper punch
Craft knife

Instructions
1. Trace pattern, transfer markings, and cut out. Using paper punch, punch out eyes.

2. Place pattern on back of art paper, trace, and transfer markings. Cut out shape with craft knife. Cut out small triangles at legs. Cut each paw slit. Lightly score fold lines and punch out eyes.

3. Fold bunnies along fold lines. Carefully interlock paws at slits. Cut ribbon into 4 equal lengths and tie each in bow around bunny's neck.

TIP

A well-promoted raffle drawing is a good way to pull in customers. The project you choose for your raffle prize will probably take more time to complete than others, so the person who makes it should start work far ahead of the bazaar date. You'll want to have the finished piece available when promoting the raffle. For more ideas, see the raffle-prize projects in each chapter of this book.

VALENTINE FAVORITES

Each of the following projects uses a different application of the traditional symbol of Valentine's Day—the heart. The little Paper Heart Basket makes a romantic party favor when filled with chocolates or other candy. The heart chain will turn a plain mantel or doorway into a valentine memory. And the dove design will win hearts when sent to a favorite valentine.

A pretty Paper Heart Basket, a romantic Dove Valentine, and a pastel Paper Chain of Hearts will give your holiday booth a touch of the sweetheart season.

Paper Heart Basket

Materials
Pattern on page 62
4" x 7" piece of art paper for hearts
⅝" x 12⅝" piece of art paper for handle
⅝" x 6½" piece of art paper for bow
⅝" x 1¾" piece of art paper for knot
White glue

Instructions
1. Trace pattern pieces, transferring markings. Cut out.
2. Place heart pattern on art paper and trace. Repeat for second heart. Trace handle, bow, and knot on art paper. Transfer markings to wrong side of art paper and cut out. Lightly score fold lines.
3. Fold tab at end of handle strip. Place small amount of glue on tab and attach to opposite end of handle strip. (Pointed fold of handle will form base of basket at heart tip.)
   Fold tabs on each side of 1 heart and apply thin layer of glue to tabs. Fit heart tip into folded base of handle, making sure that folds at tabs are even with edge of handle. Glue tabs to inside of handle. Hold together until glue dries. Repeat with second heart.
4. Apply small amount of glue to each end of bow strip. Bring ends to center, butting ends together. Allow glue to dry. Glue bow to center top of handle. Fold ends of knot strip to underside of handle and glue.

Picnic Basket Coasters

Materials for four coasters
Pattern on page 63
5" x 9" piece of red-and-white gingham
8" square of solid blue fabric
8" x 10" piece of white piqué
10" square of white terry cloth for backing
White thread
2 yards (¼"-wide) of white double-fold bias tape

Instructions
1. Trace pattern pieces F, G, H, I, and J, transferring markings. Cut out.
2. From gingham, cut 1 F. From blue fabric, cut 1 F and 2 Is. (Transfer markings to blue piece F.) From piqué, cut 1 G, 1 H, and 2 Js.
3. Clip curves on piece H (handle) and press under and baste seam allowances. Following placement line on blue piece F, appliqué piece H to blue piece F. Referring to Diagram, piece basket block. Press seams open as you work.
4. Refer to Step 4 of pot holder instructions, omitting batting, to complete coaster. Repeat to make 3 more coasters.

Picnic Basket Pot Holder

Materials
Pattern on pages 63-64
4" x 9" piece of red-and-white gingham fabric
7" x 9" piece of solid blue fabric
9" square of white piqué
8½" square of fabric for backing
White thread
3 (8½") squares of quilt batting
1¼ yards (½"-wide) of white double-fold bias tape

Instructions
1. Trace pattern pieces A, B, C, D, and E, transferring markings. Cut out.
2. From gingham, cut 1 A. From blue fabric, cut 1 A and 2 Ds. (Transfer markings to blue piece A.) From piqué, cut 1 B, 1 C, and 2 Es.
3. Clip curves on piece C (handle); press under and baste seam allowances. Following placement line on blue piece A, appliqué piece C to blue piece A. Referring to Diagram, piece basket block. Press seams open as you work.
4. Stack backing, right side down; all 3 batting squares; and basket block, right side up. Baste and then machine-stitch layers together on seam line. Bind edges with bias tape.
5. To make hanging loop, cut 6" piece from remaining bias tape. Turn under raw edges at each end of tape and whipstitch all edges closed. Fold tape in half and stitch ends to back of pot holder at top (see photograph).

Diagram: Assembling Basket Block

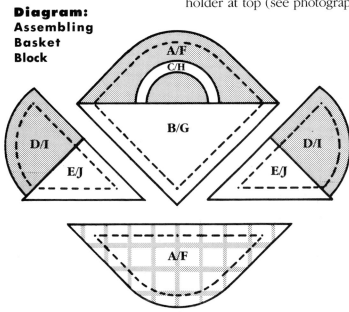

A PATRIOTIC PAIR

Scraps of red and indigo give this Celebration Star Wreath and Flag a colonial flavor. They're just right for celebrating those patriotic summer holidays: Memorial Day, July 4th, and Labor Day. And they'll help brighten summer fund-raisers, too!

TIP

Publicity is crucial to the success of your bazaar. At least a week before the event, run ads in all local newspapers. Place posters around town. If available, consider local radio and T.V. community service ads.

Celebration Star Flag

Materials
Heart Star Ornament pattern on page 144
7¼" x 10" scrap of indigo-and-white print
3½" square of antique red-and-white print
5" square of muslin
Thread to match
8½" square of paper-backed fusible web
5½" square of tear-away interfacing
16" (¼"-diameter) wooden dowel
Red wooden bead with ¼" opening
White glue
Vanishing fabric marker

Instructions
1. Trace Heart Star Ornament pattern and cut out.
2. For flag, press under ¼" hem on all edges of indigo fabric. Turn under ¼" again. Stitch hem.
3. Using marker, trace heart and star patterns on paper side of fusible web. Cut apart. Follow manufacturer's instructions to fuse heart to wrong side of red fabric and star to wrong side of muslin. Cut out each shape on outline.

Peel paper backing from star and then center star on right side of flag. Fuse in place. Peel backing from heart and fuse heart in place on star.

Baste interfacing square to wrong side of flag behind star. Zigzag-stitch along edges of star and heart. Tear away interfacing.
4. Glue wooden bead to 1 end of dowel. Glue 1 end of flag to dowel, just below bead.

Celebration Star Wreath

Materials
Pattern on page 64
2" x 36" strip of indigo-and-white print
2" x 36" strip of antique red-and-white print
Thread to match
Polyester stuffing
15" (½"-wide) of blue double-fold bias tape
Inner ring of 4"-diameter embroidery hoop
White glue
16" (⅛"-wide) of antique blue satin ribbon
4 (½") metallic paper stars
Vanishing fabric marker
Seam ripper or craft knife

Instructions
1. Trace pattern, transferring markings, and cut out.
2. With right sides facing, stitch the 2 fabric strips together along 1 long edge, using ¼" seam. Press seam open. Cut strip into 10 (3½") squares.
3. Place pattern on back of 1 pieced fabric square, with blue at top and seam on dotted line. With marker, trace heart.

With right sides facing and seams aligned, pin marked square to 1 unmarked square with same color alignment. Machine-stitch around heart on outline. Cut out heart, adding ¼" seam allowance. Clip curves and angle at top of heart and trim seam at tip.

Using seam ripper or craft knife, open ¾" of horizontal seam across center of heart on 1 side. Turn heart right side out through opening and stuff. Slipstitch opening closed. Repeat this step 4 times for total of 5 hearts.
4. With slipstitched seam at back, tack hearts together at sides where red and blue fabrics join, to form circle.

Open 1 folded edge of bias tape and enclose inner ring of hoop. Slipstitch edges closed. Spread glue on top of covered ring. Center ring on back of wreath and press to adhere. Adjust hearts to be sure open star at center is symmetrical. Let dry.
5. Tack center of ribbon to center top of wreath. Tie ends in knot to make loop. Then tie ends in bow. Glue stars to ribbon ends.

Stars and
hearts and
patriotic colors give
summer sparkle to
the Celebration Star
Flag and Celebration
Star Wreath.

47

WELCOME TO BOO CORNER

No tricks are required to make these Halloween treats. Placed on a party table or displayed at an autumn bazaar, the Candy Corn Dolls will be popular items with the ghost and goblin set (and grown ups, too). Other Halloween projects using pumpkin and bat designs will help you fill a booth with bizarre bazaar offerings.

Candy Corn Dolls (left) and a Felt Pumpkin Tote (right) make Halloween more fun for youngsters.

Candy Corn Dolls

Materials for large doll
Pattern on pages 65-66
3¼" x 9" scrap of white fabric
7" x 16" scrap of orange fabric
5" x 24" scrap of yellow fabric
5" square each of yellow and orange felt
Thread to match
Black embroidery floss
13½" (⅝"-wide) of orange grosgrain ribbon
16" (⅝"-wide) of yellow grosgrain ribbon
Fabric glue
Polyester stuffing

Materials for small doll
Pattern on pages 66-67
2¼" x 6" scrap of white fabric
4" x 9½" scrap of orange fabric
2¾" x 13½" scrap of yellow fabric
3" square each of yellow and orange felt
Thread to match
Black embroidery floss
7½" (¼"-wide) of orange grosgrain ribbon
8½" (¼"-wide) of yellow grosgrain ribbon
Fabric glue
Polyester stuffing

Instructions
Note: Instructions are the same for small and large doll.

1. On folded paper, trace pattern pieces for midsection, lower section, top, and base for doll of your choice, transferring markings. On flat paper, trace pattern pieces for foot and hand. Cut out all pieces. Seam allowances are included.

2. From white fabric, cut 2 tops. From orange fabric, cut 2 midsections. From yellow fabric, cut 1 base and 2 lower sections. From yellow felt, cut 4 feet. From orange felt, cut 4 hands.

3. Transfer facial features to right side of 1 midsection piece. Using 1 strand of floss on small face and 2 strands on large face, satin-stitch eyes, straight-stitch eyebrows, and backstitch mouth.

4. With right sides facing, join 1 top and 1 lower section to midsection with

To make the small Black Cat Magnet or Pin, use pattern on page 68 and instructions for Felt Bunny Magnet or Pin on page 10. To make Black Cat Toddler Toy, see instructions for Animal Blocks on page 96.

embroidered face to make front. Repeat with second midsection to make back, leaving opening as indicated on pattern. Press seams toward darker fabric. Staystitch along lower edge of each unit, just inside seam line.

5. To make arm, cut orange ribbon in half. Spread small amount of glue on 1 side of each of 2 hands. Sandwich ½″ of 1 end of ribbon arm between hands, aligning edges of hands. Repeat for second arm. When glue has dried, topstitch hands ¹⁄₁₆″ from edges.

6. Make legs and feet in same manner, using yellow ribbon.

7. With raw edges aligned, stitch arms and legs in position on front of doll. Fold and pin arms and legs against body to hold them in place while units are joined.

8. With right sides facing, stitch front and back units around top and sides, leaving entire lower edge open. Trim seam and clip curves. *Do not turn yet.*

Clip seam allowance almost to staystitching along lower edge of unit. With right sides facing, pin base to lower edge, matching dots on base to seams and center lines. Stitch. Trim seam and clip curves. Turn right side out, remove pins from arms and legs, and stuff doll. Slipstitch opening closed.

Felt Pumpkin Tote

Materials
Pattern on pages 67-68
11½″ x 22″ piece of black felt
11½″ x 20″ piece of orange felt
2 (1¼″ x 11″) pieces of olive felt
5″ x 11″ piece of lightweight tear-away interfacing
Thread: black, orange

2 yards (¼″-wide) of black double-fold bias tape
Vanishing fabric marker

Instructions
1. On flat paper, trace mouth and eye pattern pieces. On folded paper, trace remaining pattern pieces, transferring markings. Cut out.

2. Cut a 2″ x 11½″ strip from black felt. From this cut a mouth and 2 eyes. Set aside. On orange felt, use marker to trace 2 pumpkin shapes and 1 side/base, transferring markings. *Do not cut out these pieces yet.*

Baste eyes and mouth to front of 1 pumpkin shape, as indicated. Cut 4″ square of interfacing and baste it behind face area. Machine-appliqué eyes and mouth with black thread. Tear away excess interfacing.

3. Stack orange felt, right side up and remaining black felt. Pin layers together. Machine-stitch along outlines. Cut out all pieces, adding ¼″ seam allowances.

4. On each short end of side/base piece, trim seam allowance to ⅛″. Bind with bias tape. With black felt sides facing and dots matching, baste side/base piece to front and back pieces. Stitch. Trim seam and bind all edges with bias tape, mitering tape at center top of tote.

5. Cut strip of interfacing the same

size as olive felt strips. Place interfacing between felt strips and baste together. Bind edges with bias tape. Slipstitch ends of handle to black felt lining, being careful that stitches don't go through to outside.

Paper Pumpkin Basket

Materials
Pattern on page 69
7″ square of orange art paper
½″ x 4¾″ strip of olive art paper
White glue
Craft knife

Instructions
1. Trace pumpkin basket pattern, transferring markings, and cut out. Cut out mouth and eyes on face.

2. Trace pattern on orange paper. Cut out eyes and mouth with craft knife. Cut out basket. Lightly score fold lines.

3. Fold pumpkin along fold lines. Place small amount of glue on tabs and attach to inside back and front of pumpkin, gluing 1 tab at a time and holding in place until dry. Glue ½″ of each end of olive paper strip inside pumpkin for handle (see photograph).

Fat Bat Pot Holder

Materials

Pattern on page 70
9" x 12" piece of black pindot
    fabric
9" x 12" piece of black fabric
Purple embroidery floss
Orange heavy-duty thread
3 (9" x 12") pieces of quilt
    batting
1¼ yards (¼"-wide) of black
    double-fold bias tape
Black thread
White pencil

Instructions

1. On folded paper, trace bat pattern, disregarding grid. Transfer markings and cut out.
2. Trace pattern and markings on right side of pindot fabric using white pencil. *Do not cut out yet.* Using 1 strand of purple floss, satin-stitch eyes. Using 1 strand of orange thread, back-stitch mouth.
3. Stack black fabric; batting; and pindot fabric, right side up. Baste. Using orange thread, topstitch bat as marked. Cut out, adding ¼" seam allowance.
4. Bind pot holder with bias tape, allowing orange topstitching to show. Take tucks in tape where needed. For hanging loop, cut 5" length of bias tape. Stitch long edge closed and turn under raw ends. Fold in half and tack to center bottom on back.

Fat Bat Place Mat

Materials

Pattern on page 70
13" x 18½" piece of black pindot
    fabric
13" x 18½" piece of black fabric
Purple embroidery floss
Orange heavy-duty thread
13" x 18½" piece of quilt batting
1⅔ yards (¼"-wide) of black
    double-fold bias tape
Black thread
White pencil

Instructions

1. To enlarge bat pattern refer to Supplies and Techniques.
2. Refer to Steps 2-4 for Fat Bat Pot Holder above, using 2 strands of floss to embroider eyes. Omit loop.

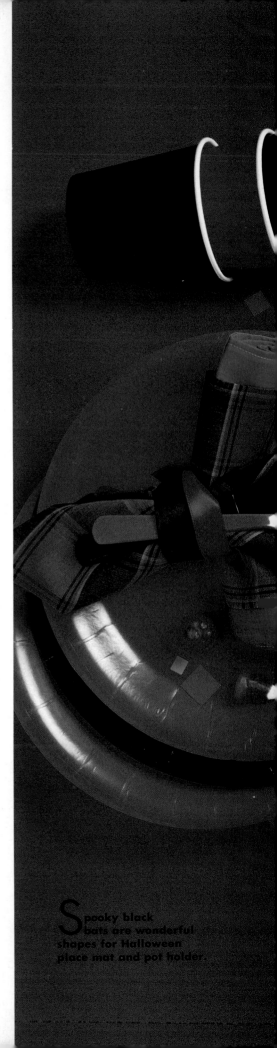

Spooky black bats are wonderful shapes for Halloween place mat and pot holder.

AUTUMN LEAVES

Classic oak leaf and acorn designs bring thoughts of the crisp days of autumn, football games, and Thanksgiving dinner. But these three projects will be hits at a bazaar any time of year.

Oak Leaf Pot Holders

Materials for one pot holder
Pattern on page 71
8″ x 12″ scrap of fabric for leaf front
8″ x 12″ scrap of fabric for leaf back
8″ x 12″ piece of thick quilt batting
1½ yards (¼″-wide) of double-fold bias tape
Thread to match tape
Vanishing fabric marker

Instructions
1. On folded paper, trace oak leaf pattern and cut out.
2. Using marker, trace leaf shape on right side of leaf front fabric. *Do not cut out yet.*
3. Stack leaf back fabric, right side down; batting; and leaf front fabric, right side up. Machine-stitch layers together on outline. Also stitch down center of leaf. Add row of ⅛″-wide zigzag stitches just outside outline of leaf. Cut out leaf just outside zigzag stitches.
4. Cut 11″ length of bias tape. Open out center fold of tape and trim 1 folded edge, cutting ⅛″ from fold, to reduce bulk. Slipstitch trimmed tape down center of leaf, using bias tape placement line as guide. Bind edges of pot holder with bias tape, beginning at bottom of leaf. Bring end of tape around to back of leaf and slipstitch in place to form loop.

Acorn Pincushions

Materials for one pincushion
Pattern on page 71
3½″ x 10″ scrap of solid brown fabric
5″ square of brown print fabric
Thread to match
Polyester stuffing
2⅛″ (¼″-wide) of brown grosgrain ribbon
Vanishing fabric marker
Pencil

Instructions
1. Trace acorn and cap pattern pieces, transferring markings. Cut out.
2. Fold solid fabric in half, right sides facing, and pin together. Trace acorn shape on 1 side. With marker, transfer markings to wrong side of fabric, letting markings soak through to right side of fabric. Machine-stitch along deep curved edge of acorn, beginning and ending stitching ¼″ beyond pattern seam line. Cut out shape, adding ⅛″ seam allowance. Clip curves.

Run row of gathering stitches by hand on seam line around open edge of acorn. Press seam allowance to wrong side and baste. Turn acorn right side out and stuff firmly. Pull thread, leaving ½″ opening. Add more stuffing. Pull thread tight and tie off. Smooth out any puckers below cap placement line.
3. To make button at base of acorn, using unknotted doubled thread, insert needle into acorn at stitching line, leaving thread tail. Make row of tiny running stitches on stitching line. Pull both ends of thread tightly to create button. Take a few stitches; then tie off.
4. Cut print fabric in half. With right sides facing, pin fabric pieces together. Stitch seam ¼″ from 1 edge, leaving 1″ open at center. Press seam open. Center and mark cap pattern on wrong side of fabric, aligning seam and opening with pattern markings. Cut out cap, adding ¼″ seam allowance. Machine-baste on outline. Clip seam allowance to basting. Press and baste seam allowance to wrong side of cap. Pull bobbin thread of basting stitches to gather cap slightly. Fit cap over acorn, matching seam lines. Seam line of cap should just cover cap placement line on acorn. Pull bobbin thread so cap fits snugly around top of acorn. Slipstitch cap to acorn.

5. Stuff cap firmly, using broken tip of pencil to push stuffing towards gathers. Flatten top of cap. Insert cut ends of ribbon in cap opening. Stitch opening closed.

Paper Leaf Wreath

Materials
Pattern on page 72
7½″ x 18″ piece of brown art paper
20 (3½″) squares of art paper in fall colors
White glue
Small piece of yarn
Craft knife
Paper punch

Instructions
1. Trace pattern pieces for leaf and wreath base. Transfer markings and cut out.
2. Using pattern, trace 4 wreath base pieces on brown paper. Cut out. Score and sharply crease fold line on each. With craft knife, cut V slits. Glue the 4 pieces together at glue tabs to form ring.
3. Trace 1 leaf on each of the 20 squares of colored paper. Cut out. Clip slits at bases of leaves as shown on pattern.

Score and fold each leaf on fold lines, bending sides of leaf back at center fold to form "mountain" and sides of leaf forward at side lines to form "valleys."
4. On flat surface, place leaves in circle in color arrangement that is pleasing to you. Place spot of glue on base of each leaf and slide base of leaf into a V slit on wreath. Continue in this way until all leaves are attached to wreath base. (See photograph to overlap leaves.)
5. To hang wreath, use paper punch to make hole in base at any point where 2 sections overlap. Tie small loop of yarn in hole.

Muted **M**autumn hues highlight this group of projects: (from top to bottom) Paper Leaf Wreath, Acorn Pincushions, and Oak Leaf Pot Holders.

BUNNY BRUNCH SET

Stitch up a set of place mats just as quick as a bunny, and then use the scraps to create a pair of pudgy pot holders. There's also a pattern to make a cozy bunny to cover a teapot or a small bread basket, to keep teatime fare warm until serving.

Bunny Place Mats

Materials for four place mats
Pattern on page 74
¾ yard of green print quilted fabric (reversible)
Embroidery floss: dark green, purple, light orchid
7 yards (¼"-wide) of dark green double-fold bias tape
Thread to match

Instructions
1. To enlarge pattern, refer to Supplies and Techniques.
2. Refer to Steps 2, 3, and 5 for Bunny Pot Holder, on this page, using 2 strands of floss for all embroidery. (See Diagram 1 to transfer bunny facial features.)

Bunny Pot Holder

Materials for one pot holder
Pattern on page 73
11" square of green print quilted fabric
11" square of Teflon-coated fabric (or another square of quilted fabric) for backing
Embroidery floss: dark green, purple, light orchid
11" square of thick quilt batting
1⅛ yards (¼"-wide) of dark green double-fold bias tape
Thread to match

Instructions
1. Trace pattern, transferring markings. Cut out.
2. From quilted fabric, cut 1 pot holder. Do not add seam allowance. Transfer facial features and bow from pattern to right side of fabric.
3. Using 2 strands of floss, satin-stitch eye dark green and chainstitch bow purple. Using 1 strand of light orchid floss, satin-stitch nose and chainstitch mouth. (All embroidery is through top layer of fabric only.)
4. Stack Teflon-coated fabric, right side down; batting; and bunny piece, right side up. Baste layers together. Trim backing fabric and batting to match quilted bunny. Stitch all layers together just inside bias tape placement line.
5. With bias tape, bind pot holder.

Diagram 1:
Actual Size Embroidery Details for Place Mat

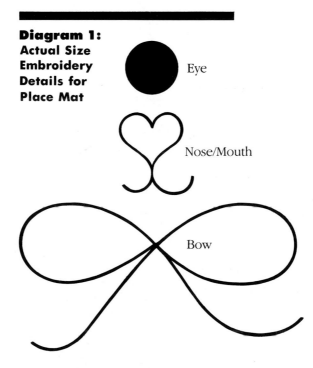

Eye

Nose/Mouth

Bow

Bunny Tea Cozy

Materials

Pattern on page 75
½ yard of green print quilted fabric
Embroidery floss: dark green, purple, light orchid
2 yards (¼″-wide) of dark green double-fold bias tape
Thread to match

Instructions

1. To enlarge pattern, refer to Supplies and Techniques. (Small cozy covers 24-ounce pot. Large cozy covers 40-ounce pot.)
2. From quilted fabric, cut 2 bunnies. Reverse pattern and cut 2 more. Do not add seam allowances. Transfer facial features and bow from Diagram 2 to right side of 1 bunny.
3. Referring to Step 3 of Bunny Pot Holder, page 54, embroider bunny features, using 2 strands of floss for all embroidery.
4. To make front of tea cozy, stack embroidered shape and 1 plain shape with wrong sides facing. Stitch along all edges. Bind bottom edge only with bias tape. Repeat with 2 remaining shapes to make back of cozy.
5. With wrong sides facing and edges aligned, stitch front and back pieces together, using ¼″ seam, and leaving bound bottom edges open. Trim seam. Bind raw edges with bias tape.

Diagram 2:
Actual Size
Embroidery
Details for
Tea Cozy

 Eye

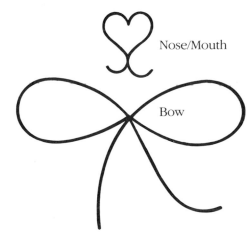

Nose/Mouth

Bow

Pretty prequilted fabric and purchased bias binding make quick work of this Bunny Tea Cozy, as well as its companions on the preceding page.

TIPS

There are a myriad of things to remember and details to work out when planning a bazaar. Here are a few suggestions you might want to consider when making plans for the big event.

•

Contact your fire department for a list of safety code requirements.

•

Call your police department well ahead of time to arrange for help with traffic control if you think you will need it.

•

Plan a play corner or inexpensive baby-sitting service, manned by volunteers, where parents can drop off their children while shopping.

•

Arrange to rent a helium tank and purchase a supply of balloons. You might even be able to get balloons, imprinted with an endorsement or advertisement, donated by a local political candidate or business.

•

A public address system for a large bazaar, or a small microphone system for a small one, will let you announce lost-and-founds and special events. It can also be used to pipe pretty seasonal music to your customers. This adds an especially nice touch to a Christmas bazaar.

•

If your bazaar is to be held a great distance from town, you might want to arrange a transportation system: chartered buses for a very large event or private cars, driven by volunteers, for a smaller one.

•

About a month before the date of your bazaar, contact local radio and T.V. stations. It might be possible to schedule a live broadcast or an interview with your chairperson.

•

Invite your mayor or other local dignitary. If your community boasts a celebrity citizen, extend an invitation to her or him. Even a brief appearance by someone famous could lure customers from surrounding communities.

Calico Eggs and
Funny Bunnies

Instructions are on page 36.

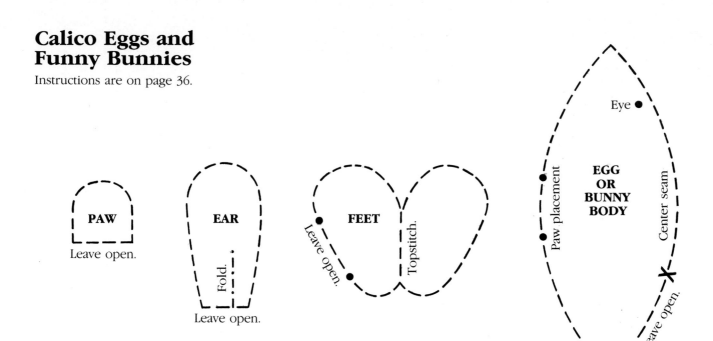

PAW

Leave open.

EAR

Fold.

Leave open.

FEET

Leave open.

Topstitch.

Eye ●

Paw placement

EGG
OR
BUNNY
BODY

Center seam

Leave open.

Soft Basket

Instructions are on page 36.

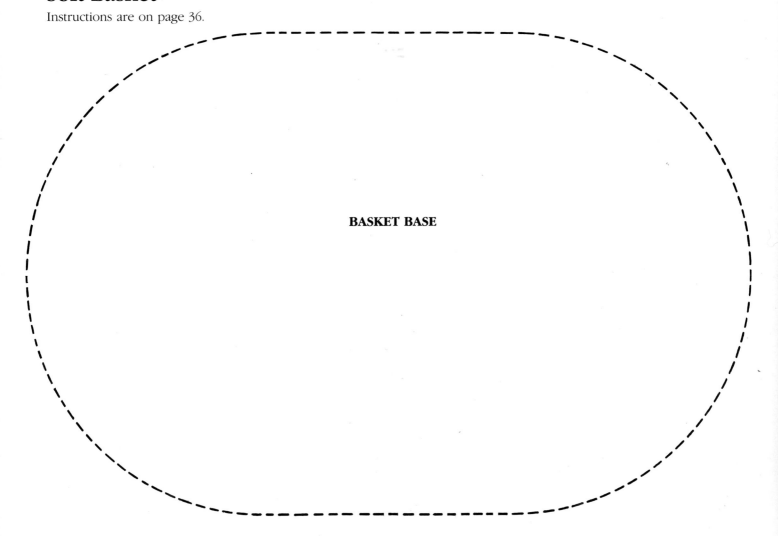

BASKET BASE

Place on fold of paper.

BASKET SIDE

Place on fold
of paper.

BASKET HANDLE

Fuzzy Bunny Bib

Instructions are on page 38.

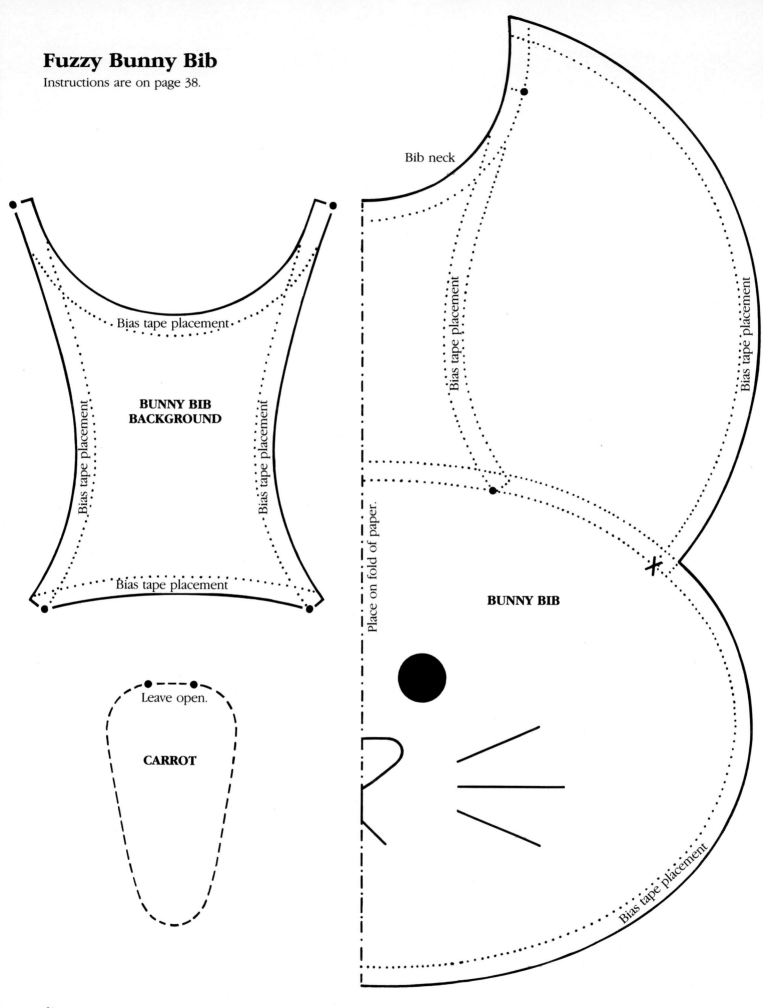

Bib neck

Bias tape placement

Bias tape placement

Bias tape placement

BUNNY BIB BACKGROUND

Bias tape placement

Bias tape placement

Bias tape placement

Place on fold of paper.

BUNNY BIB

Leave open.

CARROT

Bias tape placement

Paper Bunny Basket

Instructions are on page 39.

BUNNY BASKET

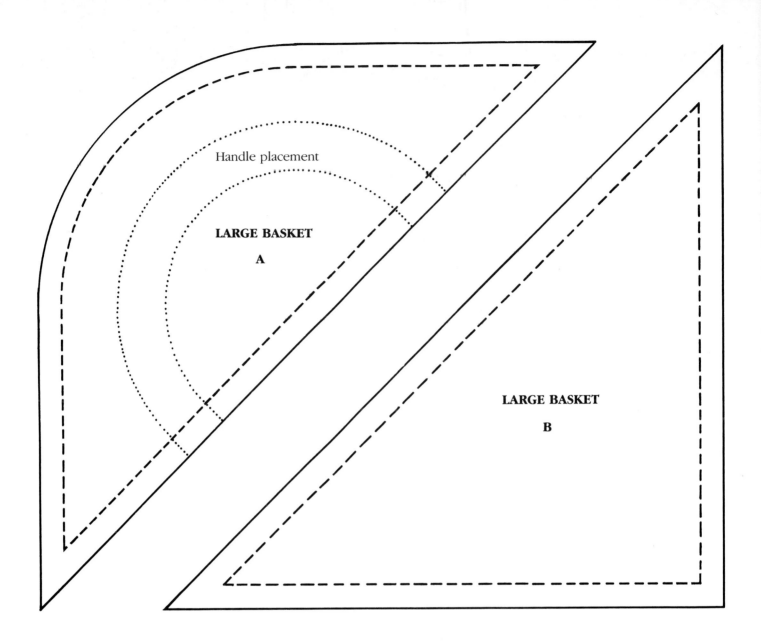

Handle placement

LARGE BASKET

A

LARGE BASKET

B

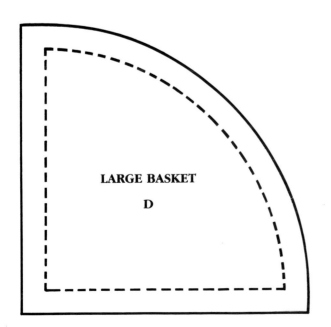

LARGE BASKET

D

Celebration
Star Wreath

Instructions are on page 46.

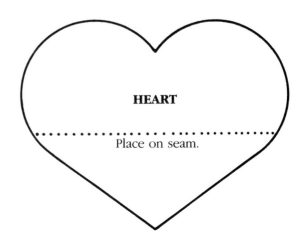

HEART

Place on seam.

Candy Corn Dolls
Instructions are on pages 48-49.

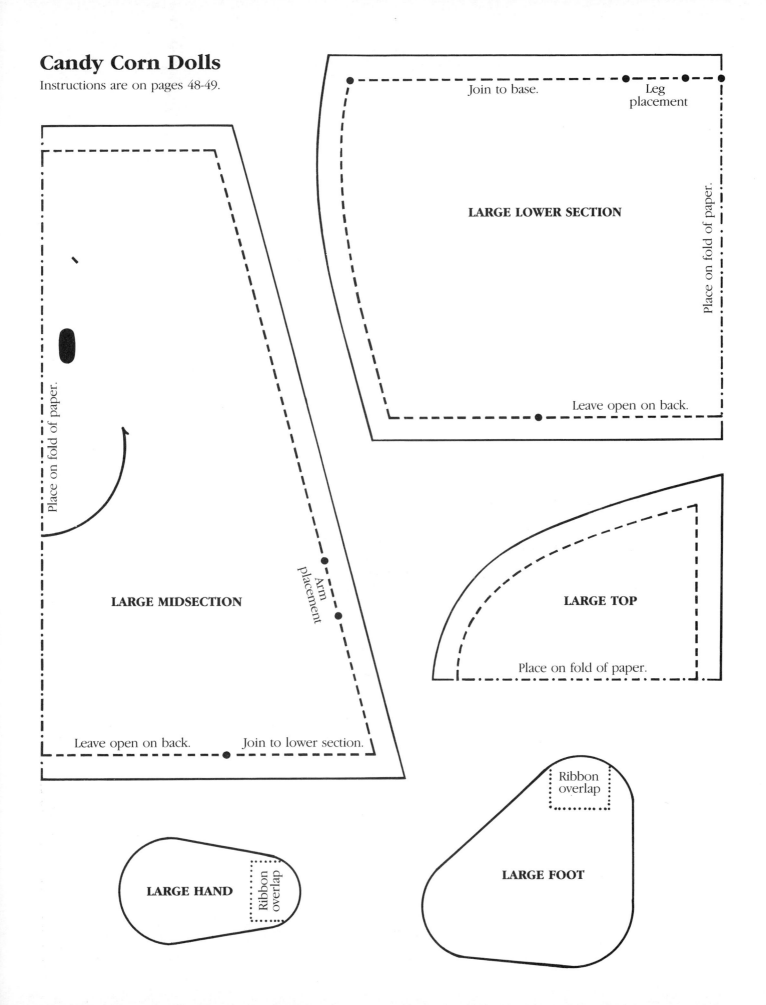

Join to base.   Leg placement

LARGE LOWER SECTION

Place on fold of paper.

Leave open on back.

Place on fold of paper.

LARGE MIDSECTION

Arm placement

Leave open on back.   Join to lower section.

LARGE TOP

Place on fold of paper.

Ribbon overlap

LARGE FOOT

LARGE HAND

Ribbon overlap

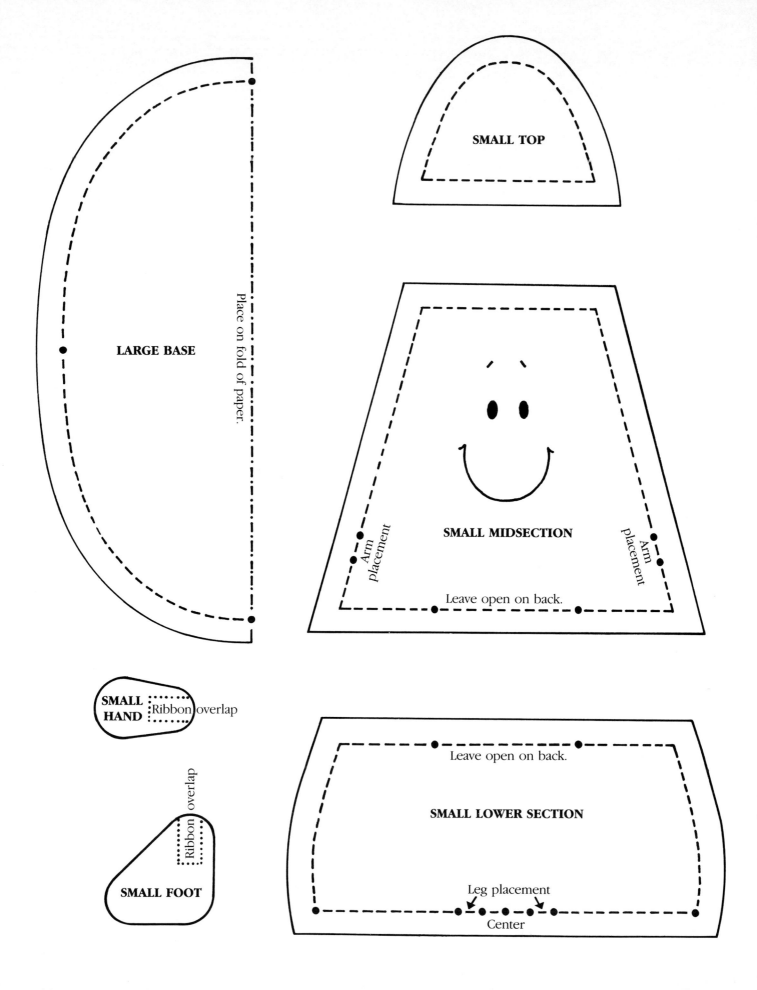

LARGE BASE

Place on fold of paper.

SMALL TOP

SMALL MIDSECTION

Arm placement

Arm placement

Leave open on back.

SMALL HAND

Ribbon overlap

SMALL FOOT

Ribbon overlap

SMALL LOWER SECTION

Leave open on back.

Leg placement

Center

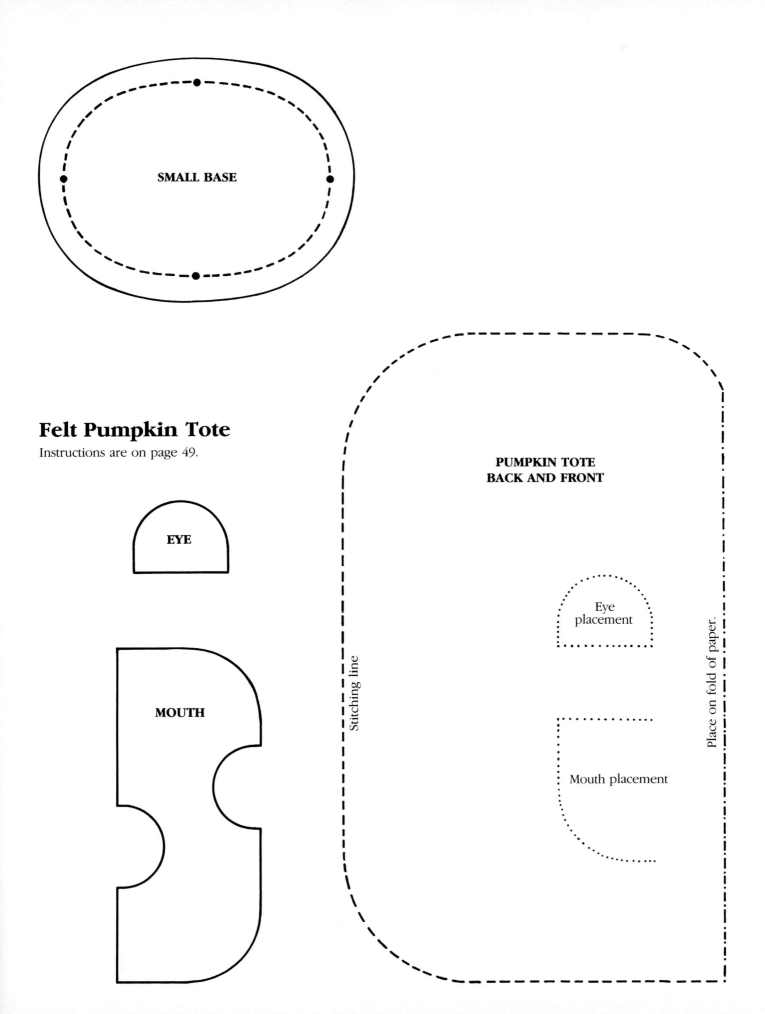

SMALL BASE

Felt Pumpkin Tote

Instructions are on page 49.

EYE

MOUTH

Stitching line

PUMPKIN TOTE
BACK AND FRONT

Eye placement

Mouth placement

Place on fold of paper.

Place on fold of paper.

**PUMPKIN TOTE
SIDE/BASE**

Black Cat
Magnet or Pin

Follow instructions for Felt Bunny Magnet or Pin on page 11, omitting embroidery.

BLACK CAT

Paper Pumpkin Basket

Instructions are on page 49.

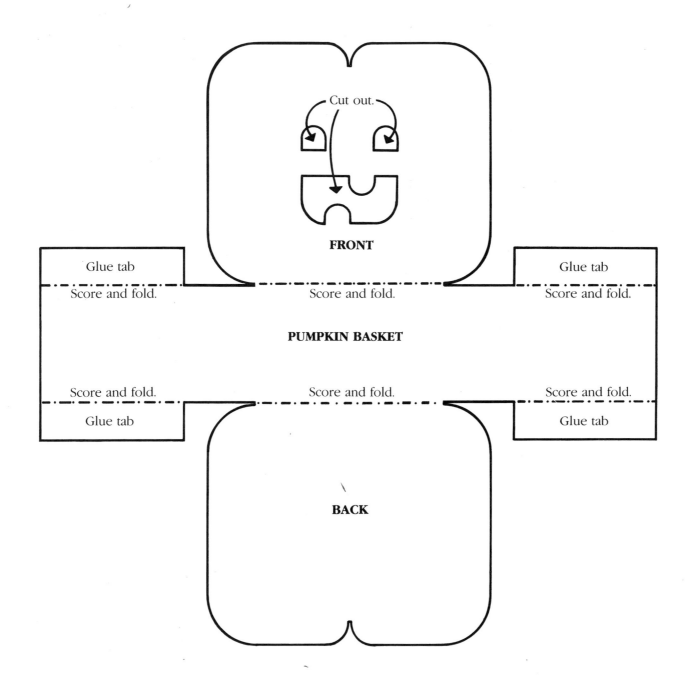

Cut out.

FRONT

Glue tab

Score and fold.

Score and fold.

Score and fold.

PUMPKIN BASKET

Score and fold.

Score and fold.

Score and fold.

Glue tab

Glue tab

Glue tab

BACK

Fat Bat Pot Holder
and Place Mat

Instructions are on page 50.

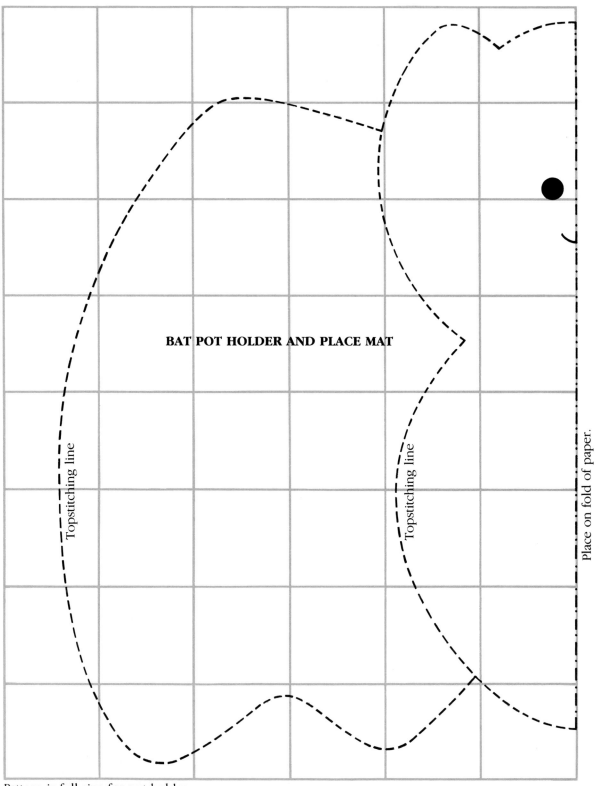

BAT POT HOLDER AND PLACE MAT

Topstitching line

Topstitching line

Place on fold of paper.

Pattern is full-size for pot holder.
Each square = 1⅝″ for place mat.

To enlarge pattern for place mat, refer to Supplies and Techniques.

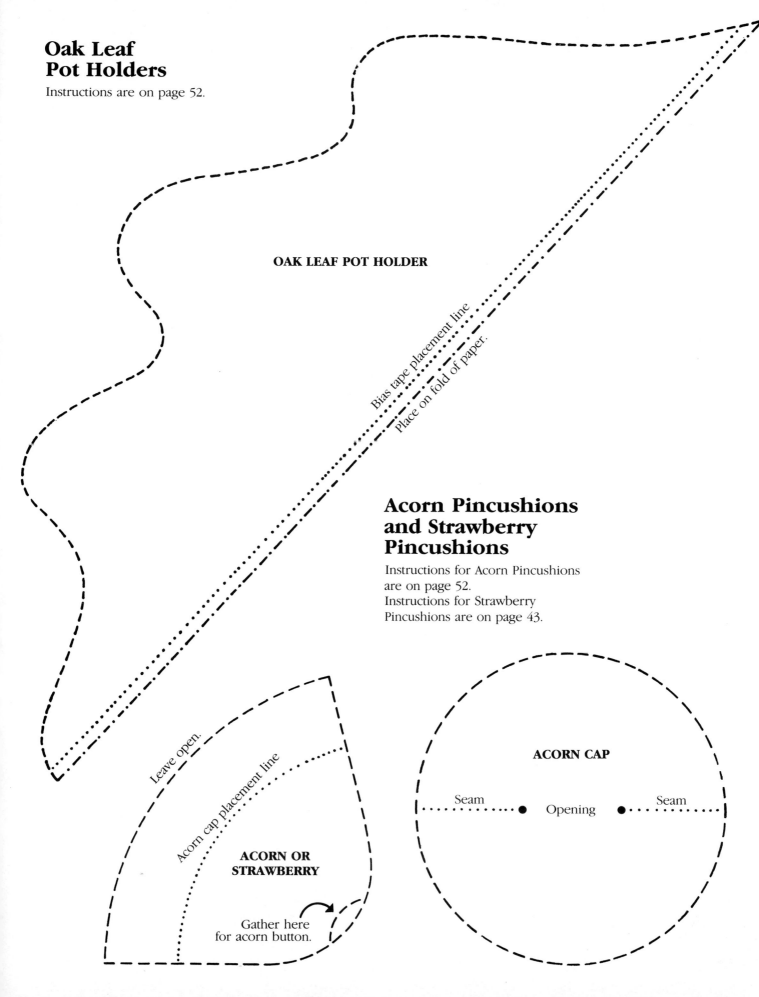

Oak Leaf
Pot Holders

Instructions are on page 52.

OAK LEAF POT HOLDER

Bias tape placement line

Place on fold of paper.

Acorn Pincushions
and Strawberry
Pincushions

Instructions for Acorn Pincushions
are on page 52.
Instructions for Strawberry
Pincushions are on page 43.

Leave open.

Acorn cap placement line

**ACORN OR
STRAWBERRY**

Gather here
for acorn button.

ACORN CAP

Seam   ●   Opening   ●   Seam

Paper Leaf Wreath

Instructions are on page 52.

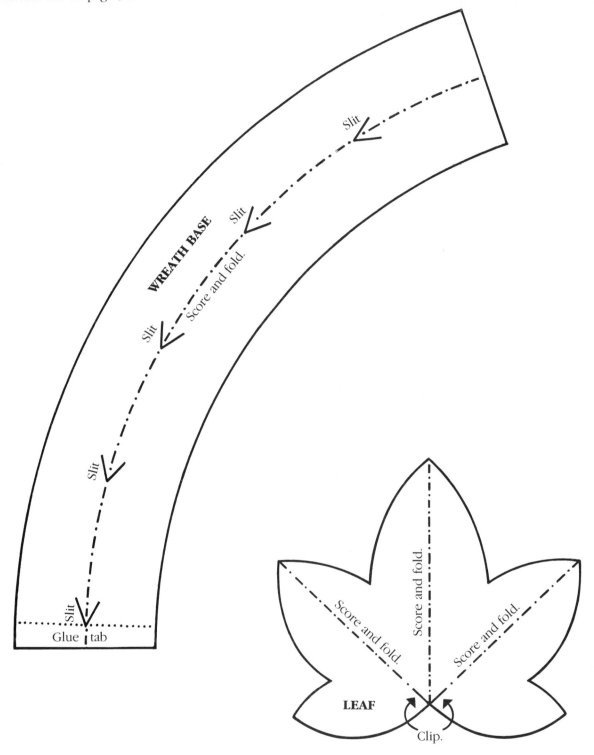

WREATH BASE

Slit

Slit

Slit

Slit

Score and fold.

Slit

Glue tab

LEAF

Score and fold.

Score and fold.

Score and fold.

Clip.

Bunny Pot Holder

Instructions are on page 54.

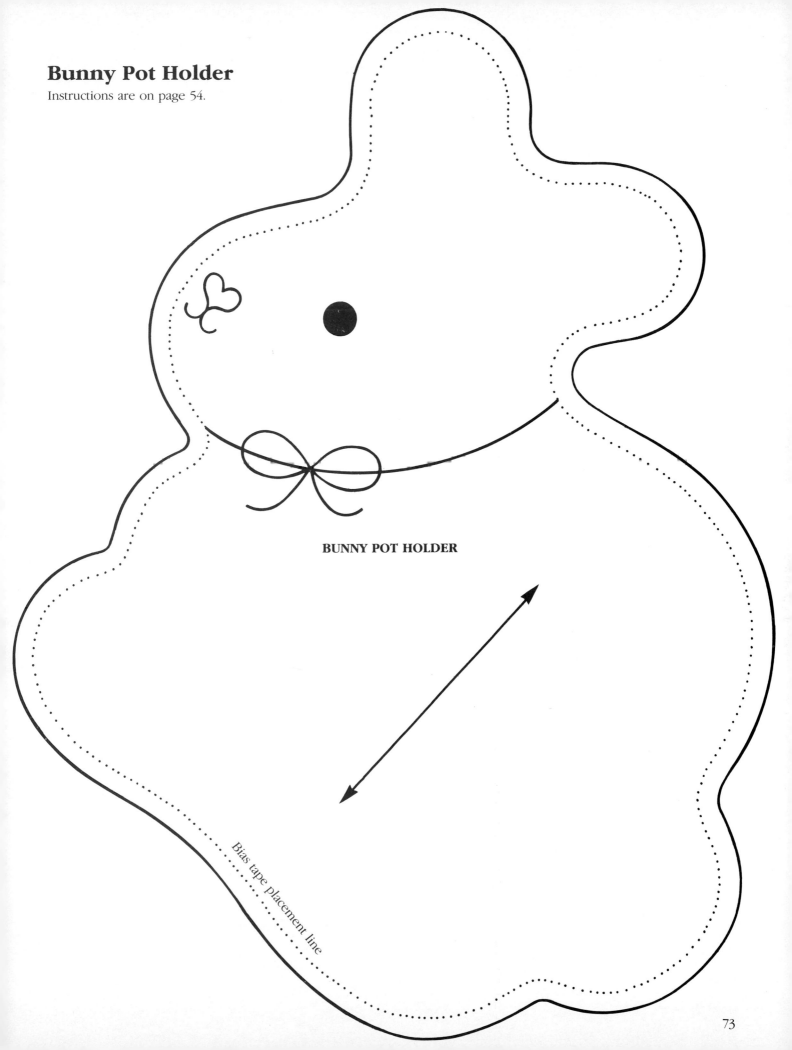

BUNNY POT HOLDER

Bias tape placement line

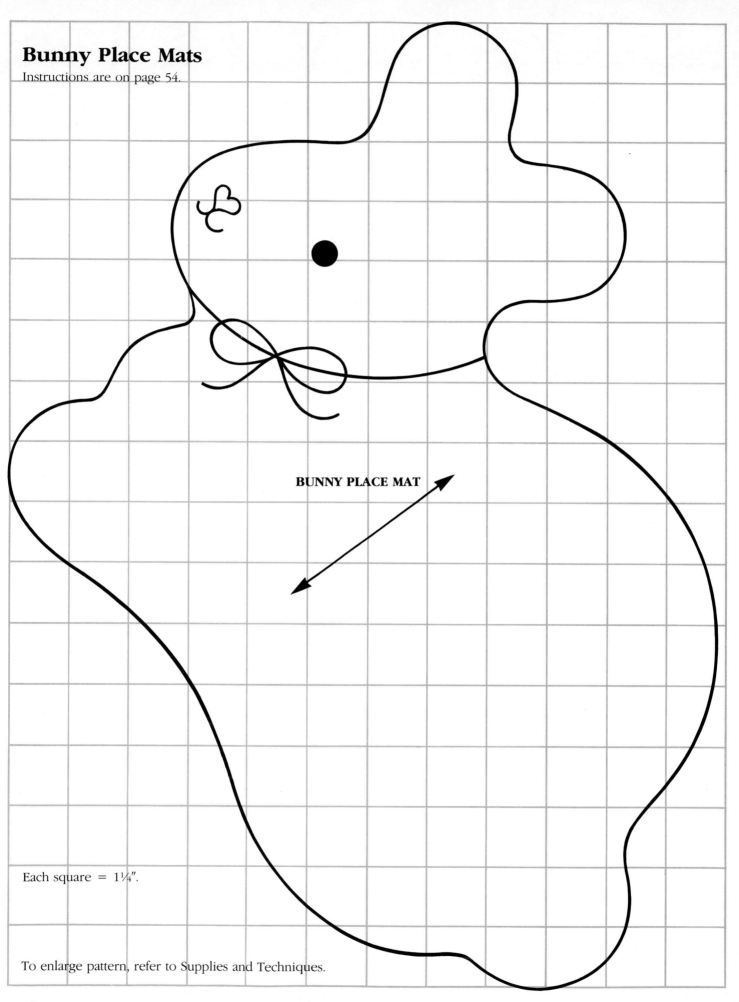

Bunny Place Mats

Instructions are on page 54.

BUNNY PLACE MAT

Each square = 1¼".

To enlarge pattern, refer to Supplies and Techniques.

Bunny Tea Cozy

Instructions are on page 56.

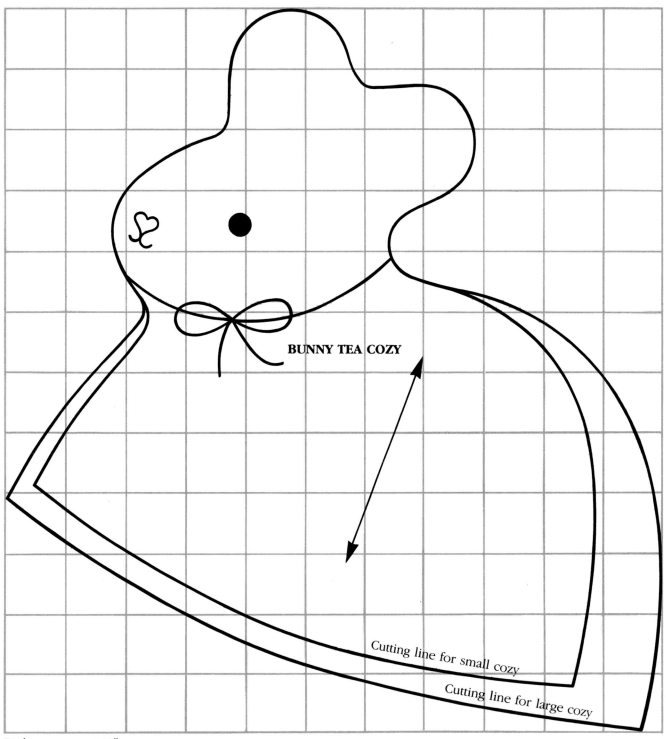

BUNNY TEA COZY

Cutting line for small cozy

Cutting line for large cozy

Each square = 1¼″.

To enlarge pattern, refer to Supplies and Techniques.

CHILDREN'S CORNER

Want to find bears, dolls, **toys,** or bibs? They're all here in this chapter, along with bright-smile surprises as well. Some designs are just **perfect** for babies, toddlers, or mothers-to-be. Others make great just-for-fun **gifts** for children of all ages.

BAZAAR BEARS

These soft and floppy teddy toys could be "beary" hot items at your next fund-raising event. Quilters will recognize the Bear Paw block on Bear Paw Papa's tummy and the Variable Star block on Star Cub. The same basic patterns can be used to make Bandanna Bear Mama and Bandanna Cubby.

The tiny Tooth Beary Twins on page 86, clad in cozy flannel, have pockets on the front of their jammies, perfect compartments for tooth fairy deliveries. Add a matching toothbrush for a clever gift that kids will love.

This family of bears is clothed in quilt blocks and bandannas. From left, Star Cub, Bear Paw Papa, Bandanna Bear Mama, and Bandanna Cubby.

General Instructions for All Bears

1. Select bear that you wish to make. Trace pattern pieces, transferring markings. Cut out.

2. Refer to materials list and instructions for bear of your choice, completing all steps required for cutting fabric, creating face, etc. Then follow Steps 3-6 below to complete your bear.

3. With right sides facing, sew head back and front together, leaving straight edge open. Trim seams, clip curves, and clip angles at ears. Turn head right side out.

Stuff ears loosely. Machine-stitch through all layers on topstitching lines of ears. Set head aside.

4. With right sides facing, pin 2 arm pieces together. Machine-stitch, leaving straight edge open. Repeat for second arm. Trim seams, clip curves, and turn arms right side out. Stuff arms and baste edges closed. Repeat Step 4 to make legs.

5. With right sides facing and raw edges aligned, pin 1 arm on each side of body front, with top edge of arm ¼" from top of body. Machine-stitch.

With right sides facing and raw edges aligned, pin 1 leg to each side of bottom of body front, with side seam of leg ¼" from side of body front. (Legs will overlap at middle of body.) Machine-stitch.

With right sides facing and raw edges aligned, pin head face down at top of body front. Fold back of head out of the way and machine-stitch front of head only to top of body.

6. With right sides facing, and arms and legs folded towards center of body, pin body front to back. Machine-stitch around sides and bottom of body, leaving open at back of neck. Clip corners and turn bear right side out. Stuff head and body through opening at neck.

Tuck seam allowance on body top inside head. Fold under seam allowance on head. Slipstitch neck opening closed. Machine-stitch through all thicknesses on seam lines where arms, legs, and head attach to body.

Bear Paw Papa

Materials
Pattern on pages 106-108
½ yard (44"-wide) of tan print fabric
4" x 12" piece of solid tan fabric
7½" x 10½" piece of solid navy fabric
3¼" square of cream felt
1½" square of maroon felt
1" x 2" scrap of navy felt
Tan thread
Embroidery floss: navy, maroon, cream
Polyester stuffing
Vanishing fabric marker

Instructions

1. On folded paper, trace head, leg, arm, and body. On flat paper, trace muzzle, eye, nose, and patches A, B, C, and D. Transfer markings and cut out.

2. On tan print, use marker to trace 2 heads, 4 arms, 4 legs, and 1 body back. Transfer markings to head. Cut out, adding ¼" seam allowances. From felt, cut 1 cream muzzle, transferring markings, 1 maroon nose, and 2 navy eyes, with no seam allowances.

3. For Bear Paw block, cut following, adding ¼" seam allowances: from tan print, 4 As; from solid tan, 1 B and 16 Cs; from navy, 4 Bs, 16 Cs, and 4 Ds.

4. Refer to Diagram 1 to assemble Bear Paw Block for body front. Press seams open.

5. Pin muzzle, nose, and eyes to right side of head front. Using 2 strands of matching floss, blanket-stitch around each appliqué. Using 2 strands of maroon floss, chainstitch mouth.

6. Refer to Steps 3-6 of General Instructions for All Bears, to complete.

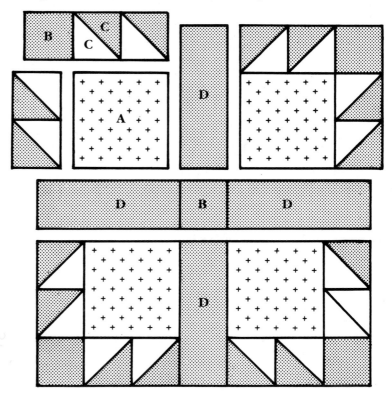

Diagram 1: Bear Paw Block Assembly

Fabric Key

Solid tan   Tan print   Solid Navy

Bandanna Bear Mama

Materials
Pattern on pages 106-107
15" x 44" piece of white fabric with black polka dots
1 large red bandanna
1 (3¼") square of felt in each of the following colors: black, white, red
Thread to match
Black embroidery floss
Polyester stuffing
34" of black medium rickrack
1 yard (⅜"-wide) of black grosgrain ribbon
12" (¼"-wide) of black grosgrain ribbon
Vanishing fabric marker

Instructions
1. On folded paper, trace head, leg, body back and front, and arm. On flat paper, trace eye, muzzle, and nose. Transfer markings and cut out.
2. On back of polka-dot fabric, use marker to trace 2 heads, 4 arms, and 4 legs. Cut out, adding ¼" seam allowances. Transfer markings.

From bandanna, cut 2 (5½" x 17") border strips for skirt. From remaining bandanna, centering design, cut 1 body front and 1 body back, adding ¼" seam allowances. From felt, cut 2 black eyes, 1 red nose, and 1 white muzzle, with no seam allowance.
3. Pin muzzle, nose, and eyes in place on right side of head front. Using 2 strands of floss, blanket-stitch around each appliqué and chainstitch mouth.
4. Refer to Steps 3-6 of General Instructions for All Bears, page 84.
5. With right sides facing and edges aligned, machine-stitch skirt pieces together along 1 short edge to make center front seam. Press seam open. Stitch ⅝" hem along 1 long edge. Sew rickrack around bottom edge, placing hem fold over center of rickrack. Narrowly hem raw edges at center back.

At top of skirt, turn under ⅝" and make row of gathering stitches close to fold. Make second row of gathering stitches ¼" from first row. Pull threads to gather top edge of skirt to 14".

Fold ⅜" ribbon in half crosswise. Place fold of ribbon on right side of skirt at center front seam. With 1 long edge of ribbon aligned with top edge

of skirt, topstitch ribbon to skirt along both ribbon edges, allowing excess ribbon to extend beyond fabric for ties. Tie skirt around bear.
6. Tie ¼" ribbon in bow and tack to 1 ear on topstitching line.

Bandanna Cubby

Materials
Pattern on pages 108-109
5" x 38" piece of white fabric with black pindots
2 (4½") squares of red bandanna with design centered
2" square of white felt
Embroidery floss: black, red
White thread
Polyester stuffing
Vanishing fabric marker

Instructions
1. On folded paper, trace head, leg, arm, and body. Trace muzzle. Transfer markings and cut out.
2. On back of pindot fabric, use marker to trace 2 heads, 4 arms, and 4 legs. Cut out, adding ¼" seam allowances. Transfer markings. Use bandanna squares for body front and back. From white felt, cut 1 muzzle.
3. Baste muzzle in place on right side of head front. With 2 strands of floss, satin-stitch eyes black and nose red. With 1 strand of black floss, blanket-stitch around muzzle and nose, and chainstitch mouth.
4. Follow Steps 3-6 of General Instructions for All Bears, page 84.

Star Cub

Materials
Pattern on pages 108-109
7" x 37" piece of solid tan fabric
3½" x 11" piece of tan print fabric
2½" x 9" piece of solid navy fabric
2" square of cream felt
Tan thread
Embroidery floss: maroon, navy, cream
Polyester stuffing
Vanishing fabric marker

Instructions
1. On folded paper, trace head, leg, arm, and body. On flat paper, trace muzzle and patches A, B, and C. Transfer all markings and cut out.
2. On solid tan, use marker to trace 2 heads, 4 arms, 4 legs, and 1 body back. Cut out pieces, adding ¼" seam allowances. From cream felt, cut 1 muzzle with no seam allowance.
3. For Star Block, cut the following pieces, adding ¼" seam allowances: from solid tan, 1 A; from tan print, 4 Bs and 8 Cs; from solid navy, 8 Cs.
4. Refer to Diagram 2 to assemble Star Block for front. Press seams open.
5. Baste muzzle in place on right side of head front. With 1 strand of maroon floss, chainstitch mouth. With 2 strands of floss, satin-stitch nose maroon and eyes navy. With 1 strand of cream floss, blanket-stitch around muzzle.
6. Refer to Steps 3-6 of General Instructions for All Bears, page 84, to complete bear.

Diagram 2: Star Block Assembly

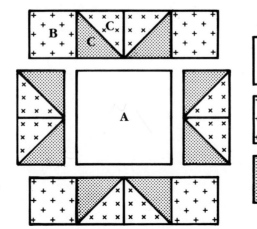

Fabric Key

Solid tan

Tan print

Solid Navy

Tooth Beary Twins

Materials for one bear and blanket

Pattern on page 109
5½″ x 10½″ piece of tan fabric
10½″ square of flannel print
1¾″ square of tan felt
9¼″ x 17½″ piece of striped flannel for blanket
Thread to match
Embroidery floss: tan, navy
Polyester stuffing
4″ (¼″-wide) of satin ribbon to match flannel print (optional)
18″ (1″-wide) of satin ribbon to match striped flannel
Child's toothbrush (optional)
Vanishing fabric marker

Instructions

1. On folded paper, trace head, arm, leg, and body. On flat paper, trace muzzle. Transfer markings and cut out.

2. Cut 1¾″ x 10½″ piece from tan fabric and 2½″ x 10½″ piece from print. With right sides facing, stitch pieces together along 1 long edge. Press seam open. On back of fabric unit, use marker to trace 4 arms ½″ apart, placing dotted line of pattern on seam line. On tan fabric, trace 2 heads ½″ apart. Cut out all pieces, adding ¼″ seam allowances. On flannel, trace 4 legs and 3 body pieces ½″ apart. From tan felt, cut 1 muzzle.

3. Pin muzzle in place on right side of head front. With 1 strand of tan floss, blanket-stitch around muzzle. With 2 strands of navy floss, satin-stitch eyes and nose. With 1 strand of navy floss, chainstitch mouth.

4. To make pocket, fold 1 (3½″) flannel square in half, wrong sides facing, and baste to bottom half of second flannel square, aligning raw edges. Then machine-stitch center of pocket from top to bottom to make 2 pockets.

5. Follow Steps 3-6 of General Instructions for All Bears, page 84. Tie ¼″ ribbon in bow and tack to bear's ear at topstitching (optional).

6. To make blanket, fold striped flannel in half crosswise with right sides facing. Stitch ¼″ seam along side opposite fold. Turn blanket right side out. Press. Cut 1″ ribbon in half and bind open ends of blanket.

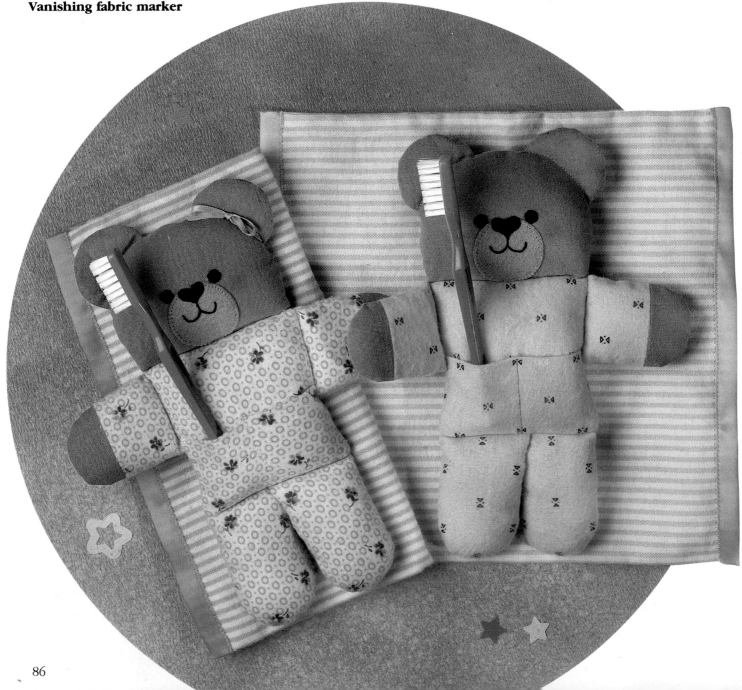

PANDA SCRUBBERS

To make these soft panda wash mitts, search for bargain washcloths. If you can't find black, substitute navy cloths with thread and felt to match. Or create a brand-new species of pastel or primary pandas.

Wash Mitt

Materials for one mitt (either size)
Patterns on pages 110-111
2 black washcloths
6″ square of white terry cloth
2″ x 3″ scrap of black felt
Embroidery floss: white, black
Thread: black, white
White pencil
Vanishing fabric marker

Instructions
1. On folded paper, trace mitt and face of your choice, transferring markings. On flat paper, trace eye patch. Transfer chainstitch line. Cut out.

2. Pin mitt pattern to 1 washcloth, placing bottom edge of pattern along finished edge of cloth. With white pencil, trace around pattern and transfer face placement line. Cut out, adding ¼″ seam allowance. Repeat for panda back, omitting face placement line.

3. Pin face pattern to right side of white terry cloth. With marker, trace pattern and transfer eye, nose, and mouth placement lines. *Do not cut out yet.* Pin eye patch pattern to black felt and trace, transferring chainstitch line. Reverse pattern and repeat.

With 1 strand of white floss, chainstitch circles on eye patches. Cut out eye patches on outline and baste in place on face. Machine-zigzag around each patch, using black thread. With 1 strand of black floss, chainstitch mouth and backstitch around nose. With 2 strands of black floss, satin-stitch nose.

Cut out face, adding ¼″ seam allowance. Clip curves. Turn under seam allowance and baste. Baste face in place on mitt. Using white thread, appliqué face in place.

4. Lay mitt front, face down, on mitt back. With raw edges aligned, stitch mitts together along top and side edges, leaving bottom open.

Clip curves and angles at paws and ears. Turn mitt right side out. Hand-press flat. Topstitch ¼″ from seamed edge of mitt, leaving bottom open. Topstitch across base of each ear.

Two fluffy washcloths and some scraps of terry cloth, felt, and embroidery floss are all you need to create these Panda Scrubbers. They'll make bath time more fun for kids of all ages.

POCKET BABIES

To make these tiny Pocket Babies, combine your very smallest snippets of fabric, ribbon, lace, and felt. Tuck triplets into a cozy pocketed bunting for a delightful shower favor or appealing gift.

Pocket Baby

Materials for one doll
Pattern on page 112
4" x 5" scrap of pastel print fabric
1½" square of pink, tan, or brown felt for face
Thread to match
5" (⅛"-wide) of satin ribbon
Fabric glue
Embroidery floss: pink, blue, brown, yellow, black
Powder blush
Cotton swab
Polyester stuffing
7½" (¼"-wide) of flat lace
Vanishing fabric marker

Diagram: Making Bow

Figure 1   Center

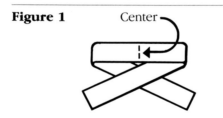

Figure 2   Stitch.

Instructions

1. Trace Pocket Baby pattern, transferring markings, and cut out.

2. Cut fabric in half to form 2 (2½" x 4") pieces. Center baby pattern on right side of 1 piece and trace around shape with marker. Transfer pattern markings to fabric. Transfer stitching line to back of fabric with basting stitches. *Do not cut out piece yet.*

3. Cut 2½" length of ribbon and glue it down center on right side of baby front as indicated on pattern.

4. On felt, trace 1 face. Transfer either waking face or sleeping face features to felt with pencil or marker. Using 2 strands of floss in desired colors, make French knots for waking eyes and straight stitches for mouth and sleeping eyes. Brush a little blush on cheeks with cotton swab. Cut out face, pin in place, and appliqué to baby front.

5. With right sides facing, pin baby front to remaining fabric piece. Machine-stitch around shape, leaving opening as indicated. Trim seam allowance to ¼". Clip curves and turn right side out. Stuff baby firmly. Slipstitch opening closed.

6. To make hair, use 1 strand of floss in desired color. Take 4 or 5 small stitches at top center of face at seam line, leaving ½" thread loops between stitches and taking 1 backstitch between every 2 loops to lock them. Clip loops and trim to desired length.

Gather lace to fit circumference of baby's face. Pin lace around outside of baby's face, with cut ends meeting at bottom center of face. Turn cut ends under and slipstitch lace in place.

To make bow, mark center of remaining ribbon, then fold each end toward center as in Figure 1 of Diagram. Take stitch at center through all ribbon layers as in Figure 2. Wrap thread around bow center 2 or 3 times and tie off. Tack bow in place at baby's chin.

Pocket Bunting

Materials
Pattern on page 112
6½″ x 9½″ scrap of pastel print fabric for bunting
6½″ x 9½″ scrap of pastel dot fabric for lining
6½″ x 9½″ scrap of felt or flannel
26″ (¼″-wide) of double-fold bias tape
18″ (¼″-wide) of satin ribbon
Thread to match
Vanishing fabric marker

Instructions
1. Trace Pocket Bunting pattern, transferring markings. Cut out.

2. On right side of bunting fabric, center bunting pattern. Use marker to trace bunting shape. *Do not cut out yet.* Layer lining fabric, right side down; felt; bunting fabric, right side up. Pin layers together and stitch all the way around outline. Cut out, adding ³⁄₁₆″ seam allowance.

3. Cut 9″ length of bias tape and bind long straight edge of bunting. With lining sides facing, fold fabric on fold line and pin. Baste sides of pocket to sides of bunting. Bind remaining edges with bias tape, tucking under cut ends of tape. Topstitch both sets of double lines through all layers, as indicated on pattern, to make 3 pockets.

Fold ribbon in half to find center. Tack center of ribbon to center back of Pocket Bunting. Tuck Pocket Baby in each pocket, fold outer pockets to center, and tie ribbon ends in bow.

Even the smallest bits of fabric in your scrap bag can be put to good use to make a bunting full of Pocket Babies.

PATCHWORK TOYS

There's nothing subtle about the six bright and brassy crayon colors stitched together in these toddler toys. To make each patchwork square tell its own color story, start with a basic brilliant hue and then add one medium and one light print. The six basic patchwork squares can be used to make any or all of the following projects—block, book, or boa.

The Pencil Apron uses the same colors for a cover-up that's practical and fun to wear.

Pencil Apron

Materials
Pattern on pages 113-114
16″ x 26″ piece of black fabric
4″ x 16″ piece of tan fabric
6″ x 26″ piece each of red, yellow, and blue fabric
Thread to match
62½″ (1″-wide) of black cotton twill tape
1 set of (1″) D rings

Instructions
1. Trace pattern, transferring markings. Cut out. Cut out 1 (5¼″ x 12″) rectangle and label it pattern piece E. Cut 1 (5¼″ x 10″) rectangle and label it pattern piece F.

2. Cut a 16″ x 19″ piece of black fabric and set aside for backing. From remaining black fabric, cut 1 A and 2 Bs. From tan fabric, cut 3 Cs. From each of the 3 colored fabrics, cut 1 D, 1 E, and 1 F.

3. Refer to Diagram and arrange pieces right side up on work surface. Press all seams open as you go. To make Unit 1, stitch a colored D to a tan C. Repeat twice to make 3 Unit 1 pieces. Join them by stitching Bs between units as in Diagram. Stitch piece A across top of D/C/B piece.

To make Unit 2, fold 1 F in half crosswise, wrong sides facing. With right sides facing and raw edges aligned, pin folded F to 1 end of E of same color. Baste together along the 3 raw edges to make a pocket. Repeat to make 2 more Unit 2 pieces.

Stitch Unit 2 pieces together as shown in Diagram, in same color sequence as Unit 1 pieces. Stitch Unit 1 to Unit 2 as shown in Diagram.

4. Cut twill tape into 3 (20″) lengths and 1 (2½″) length. To make waist ties, with right sides facing and raw edges aligned, stitch 1 (20″) length of tape to each side of apron front where indicated in Diagram.

To make neck strap, with right sides facing and raw edges aligned, stitch remaining 20″ of tape to upper left side of apron bib. Run the short piece of tape through both D rings. With right sides facing and raw edges aligned, stitch both ends of loop to upper right side of apron bib.

5. With straps resting on apron front, right sides facing, and side and bottom edges aligned, pin black apron backing to front. Stitch edges, leaving 4″ opening along 1 edge. (Be careful not to catch straps in seams.) Trim backing fabric at top, clip corners, and turn apron right side out. Press. Slipstitch opening closed. Machine-stitch "in the ditch" on seam lines between pencils. Hem raw ends of twill tape.

Diagram: Assembling apron front

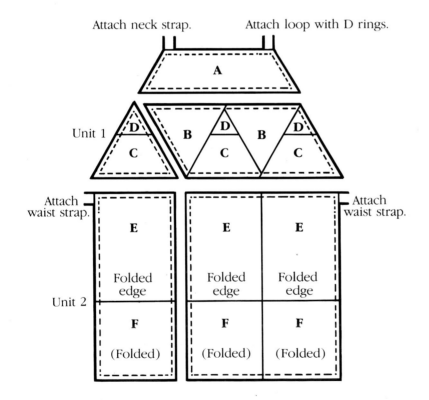

Three enormous colored pencils brighten the front of this cover-up apron for young artists. Bright patchwork adorns the large boa, the large block, and the fabric book. And matching colors make up the small boa and small blocks.

Patchwork Boa

Materials

Pattern on page 115
1 set of 6 completed Patchwork
  Squares (see page 92)
1 (6½″) fabric square in each of
  the following solid colors:
  blue, red, and orange
8″ x 21″ piece of solid yellow
  fabric
8″ x 21″ piece of solid green
  fabric
8″ x 15″ piece of red with white
  miniprint fabric
8″ x 12″ piece of solid purple
  fabric
Thread to match
1 yard of white jumbo rickrack
Polyester stuffing
2 (1″) black shank buttons
(*Note*: If toy is for small child,
  substitute black embroidery floss
  for buttons and satin-stitch eyes.)

Instructions

1. On folded paper, trace pattern
pieces E and F, transferring markings.
Cut out.
2. Cut pieces from fabric as indicated
on pattern. Cut 1 (6½″) square each
from yellow, green, and purple.
3. If embroidering eyes, use 2 strands
of floss to satin-stitch eyes on head. (If
using buttons for eyes, they will be
sewn on in final step.)
4. With right sides facing, stitch patchwork squares together as shown in
photograph. Add green head with eyes
to green square and yellow tail to
yellow square. Press seams open. To
make underbody, join solid-colored
squares in same color order as body
top, adding remaining head and tail.
5. Cut rickrack in half. On right side of
fabric, stitch rickrack around curved
edges of red print mouth pieces, centering rickrack on seam line.

With right sides facing, stitch tongue
pieces together along curved edges.
Clip curves and turn. Press. With
straight edges aligned, center and
stitch tongue to right side of 1 mouth
piece. Press and baste seam allowance
along straight edge to wrong side.

With right sides facing and curved
edges aligned, pin 1 mouth piece to
head top and 1 mouth piece to head
bottom. (Pressed straight edges of
mouth pieces should rest on seam
lines of heads.) Machine-stitch along

Yet another
application
of the patchwork
squares on page
92 is found in
Patchwork Boa
(left). The Baby
Rain-Boa (far
left) is made
from solid-colored
fabric squares and
can be stitched
up and stuffed
in no time.

curved edges. *Do not turn mouth yet.*

6. With right sides facing, pin body top and underbody together, aligning all seams. Stitch along both sides and around tail but not head. Clip curves and turn body. (Leave mouth sections wrong side out.)

7. Stuff tail. Align top and underbody seams where tail meets next square and stitch on seam line through all layers. Continue to stuff and stitch each section in this way, ending with green square.

8. Clip curves around each head/mouth unit. Turn right side out. Stuff. Slipstitch straight folded edge of mouth unit without tongue to head seam inside mouth. Slipstitch folded edge of remaining mouth unit to straight edge of first unit.

If using buttons for eyes, sew them in place as indicated on pattern.

Baby Rain-Boa

Materials

Pattern on page 115
3½″ x 7″ fabric scraps in 10 different solid rainbow colors
3½″ x 7″ scrap of magenta fabric for mouth
2½″ x 6″ scrap of solid red fabric (for tongue)
Thread to match
18″ of white medium rickrack
Polyester stuffing
2 (½″) black shank buttons
(*Note*: If toy is for small child, substitute black embroidery floss for buttons and satin-stitch eyes.)

Instructions

1. Trace pattern pieces G and H, transferring markings. Cut out.

2. Arrange 3½″ x 7″ fabric scraps in rainbow order (see photograph). Using pattern piece G, cut 2 pieces for head, 2 pieces for tail, and 2 pieces from magenta for mouth. Using piece H, cut 2 pieces from red for tongue. Cut each remaining scrap in half crosswise to make 2 (3½″) squares.

3. Refer to Step 3 of Patchwork Boa, page 94.

4. With right sides facing, stitch squares together as shown in photograph to form long strip. Stitch head to 1 end and tail to other end. Press seams open. Repeat for underbody.

5. Refer to Steps 5-8 of Patchwork Boa.

TIPS

When planning a bazaar, you'll want to consider packaging.

●

It's a good idea to prepackage candy and baked goods. Cookies can be placed in transparent bags and tied with pretty ribbon. Or use plastic bags with zip locks and adorn them with decorative labels.

●

To make candy more attractive, place it in small handmade containers, such as the Paper Bunny Basket on page 39, the Paper Pumpkin Basket on page 49, and the miniature Christmas boxes on pages 132 and 133.

●

Transparent bags, especially the kind with zip locks, are also good packaging for small craft items. You might even want to package some of your larger crafts in transparent bags to protect them from dust and the hazards of overhandling.

●

If your budget allows, lay in a supply of brown bags of varying sizes to bag purchases for customers. These can be easily decorated using purchased rubber stamps or stencils. Or make a stencil of your bazaar name and logo, if any, from a sheet of plastic quilt template material. The stencil can be used to decorate posters advertising the event, too.

PETS ON PARADE

Five baby animals march across the pages of a toddler's soft fabric book, or each animal stands alone as a foam-filled block toy, edged with colorful grosgrain ribbon.

Pet Parade Animal Blocks

Materials for one animal
Patterns on pages 116-117
6" x 12" piece of print fabric
2" x 4" piece of coordinating print fabric (for puppy's ears)
6" square of 1"-thick foam
6" x 12" piece of medium-weight fusible interfacing
2" x 4" piece of tear-away interfacing (for puppy's ears)
Black embroidery floss
Thread to match
23" (1"-wide) of matching grosgrain ribbon
2" (3/8"-wide) of grosgrain ribbon (for pig's tail)
16" (1/8"-wide) of satin ribbon
Vanishing fabric marker
Craft knife

Instructions
1. Trace patterns, transferring markings. Cut out.
2. Place pattern on foam, aligning bottom edge of animal's feet with straight edge of foam. Using marker, trace pattern. With craft knife held perpendicular to work surface, cut straight down into foam on outline. Cut shape with gentle sawing motion, cutting twice around shape, if necessary.
3. Trace 1 animal shape on side of interfacing without bonding. Reverse pattern and trace 1 more animal shape. Cut out shapes on outlines. Place shapes, bonding side down, 1/2" apart on wrong side of fabric. Following manufacturer's instructions, fuse material together. Cut out shapes, adding 1/4" seam allowance. Transfer pattern markings to right sides of shapes. (For puppy, cut 2 ears without seam allowance. Baste 1 ear to right side of each puppy. Baste 1 square of tear-away interfacing behind each ear. Zig-zag-stitch around each ear and tear

away interfacing.)
4. With 1 strand of black floss, satin-stitch eyes. Clip curves. Finger-press seam allowance to wrong side of each shape and baste in place.
5. Pin 1 fabric shape to matching side of foam, aligning edges. Starting at bottom rear, pin wide grosgrain ribbon along edge, pushing pins straight into foam. (For pig, begin and end ribbon at pig's tail position. To make tail, fold narrow grosgrain ribbon in half to form a loop. With loop pointing toward head, baste ends of ribbon in place on pig's back where wide ribbon ends join.) Turn under 1/4" at end of wide ribbon and overlap ends. Pin. Stitch edges of ribbon to shape, securing overlapped ends of ribbon. Pin remaining fabric shape to other side of foam and stitch to ribbon as above. Tie satin ribbon in bow around animal's neck.

Pet Parade Fabric Book

Materials
Patterns on pages 116-117
6½" x 13" piece of pastel print fabric for front and back covers of book
1 (6½" x 13") piece each of 5 different bright pastel print fabrics
1 (6½") square of coordinating light pastel print fabric for each bright pastel
2" square of coordinating pastel print fabric for puppy's ear
4" square of white print fabric for heart
6 (6½") squares of white flannel
½ yard of paper-backed fusible web
Thread to match
Embroidery floss: black, color to match pig
7" (½"-wide) of white double-fold bias tape
10" (1/8"-wide) of satin ribbon in each of 5 different colors to coordinate with bright pastels

Instructions
1. Trace patterns, transferring markings. Cut out.
2. From web, cut 5 (6") squares and 1 (4") square. On paper side of each 6" square, trace a different animal shape.

(Be sure to trace puppy's ear separately.) On 4" square, trace heart shape. *Do not cut out shapes yet.*
3. Cut cover fabric in half to form 2 (6½") squares. Set aside. Cut bright pastel fabrics in half to form 2 (6½") squares each.

Following manufacturer's instructions, fuse 1 web animal to wrong side of 1 bright pastel square. Continue with remaining web animals, fusing each animal to a different color square. Fuse ear to wrong side of coordinating pastel print. Transfer markings to fabric side of animal shapes. Fuse web heart to wrong side of white print square. Cut out each shape along outline.

Peel paper backing from ear. Place ear on right side of puppy shape and fuse in place where indicated on pattern. Peel paper backing from animal shapes. Center each animal, fabric side up, on front of its coordinating light pastel print square and fuse. Center heart on cover square and fuse.
4. With 1 strand of black floss, satin-stitch each animal's eye. With matching floss, chainstitch pig's tail. Using matching thread, zigzag-stitch around each shape and around puppy's ear.
5. Arrange 6 stacks of pages in this order: appliqué square, right side up; bright pastel square, right side down; and flannel square. Back cover square with fabric to match animal shape on second page. Back second page with color to match animal shape on third page. Continue backing each page with color to match following page. Back last appliquéd page with fabric to match front cover.
6. Pin layers together and machine-stitch 1/4" seam around top, right, and bottom edges, leaving left edge open. Grade seam allowances and clip corners. *Do not trim seam allowance on unstitched edges.* Turn each page right side out and press. Machine-stitch open edges together 1/8" from edge.
7. Pin pages together so that each turn of a page will reveal a single color. Machine-stitch 1/4" from raw edge through all layers. Bind raw edge of book with bias tape, tucking in ends of bias tape at top and bottom of binding.

Tie each ribbon in a bow. Tack 1 bow securely to neck of each animal.

Animal
Ablock toys
surround a soft
fabric toddler's
book. The animal
shapes are re-
peated inside the
pages of the book.

Kitten Quilt

Materials for (41″ x 61″) quilt
Pattern on pages 118-119
½ yard (45″-wide) of light print fabric
⅓ yard (45″-wide) each of bright pastel print fabric: pink, orchid, blue, green
1⅔ yards (45″-wide) of solid light brown fabric
1¾ yards (45″-wide) of light print fabric for backing
Thread to match
Embroidery floss: brown, cream, pink

1¼ yards (⅜″-wide) of satin ribbon to coordinate with each of the bright pastel fabrics
42″ x 62″ piece of quilt batting
Cream quilting thread
6 yards (½″-wide) of cream double-fold bias tape

Instructions:
1. Referring to Steps 1-4 of Kitten Tote, page 98, make 3 kitten blocks each from pink, orchid, blue, and green, for a total of 12 blocks.
2. To make sashing, from brown fabric, cut 16 (2¾″ x 11¾″) strips (piece K); cut 15 (2¾″ x 9½″) strips (piece L); cut 20 (2¾″) squares (piece M). (All sashing dimensions include ¼″ seam allowances.)

3. Join kitten blocks with sashing, following Diagram 4 for placement.
4. To make outer border, from brown fabric, cut 2 (2¾″ x 56¾″) strips, 2 (2¾″ x 36½″) strips, and 4 (2¾″) squares. Border dimensions include ¼″ seam allowance. With right sides facing and raw edges aligned, sew longer strips to each side of quilt top. Sew 1 square to each end of shorter strips; then sew strips to top and bottom of quilt top.
5. Stack backing fabric, right side down; batting; and top, right side up. Baste through all layers. Outline-quilt each piece of top ¼″ from seams through all layers (see Diagram 3). Remove basting. Bind edges of quilt with bias tape, mitering corners.

Diagram 4: Quilt Block Placement
(Diagram does not include outer border.)

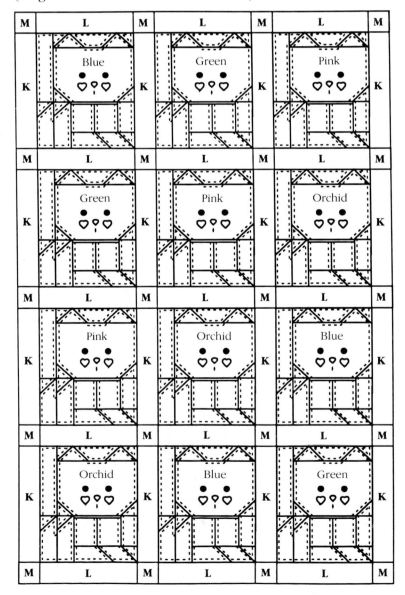

CHRISTMAS HOUSE

'Tis the night before Christmas, and all through the house, you'll find sweatshirts and stockings—even a **bright** Christmas mouse. Trim the tree with fabric and paper ornaments. Deck the halls with **festive,** easy-to-do projects. Bring handmade **joy** to a Christmas bazaar— or to your own holiday gift-giving.

GIFTS FROM SANTA

Instead of his signature, Santa's portrait adorns his designer giftware collection. Since these Santa patterns come in three sizes, this group of designs can be used for decorating trees, packages, kitchens, or even people!

Santa Pot Holder

Materials
Pattern on page 143
3″ x 5″ scrap of red print fabric
7½″ x 8½″ piece of white terry cloth
6″ square of solid pink fabric
9″ x 10½″ piece of green fabric for backing
Embroidery floss: dark green, pink, red
Thread to match
2 (9″ x 10½″) pieces of quilt batting
39″ (½″-wide) of dark green double-fold bias tape
Vanishing fabric marker

Instructions
1. On folded paper, trace patterns for large face, large beard, and large hat, transferring markings. Cut out.
2. On red fabric, use marker to trace 1 hat. On terry cloth, trace 1 beard, transferring placement line. Cut out pieces, adding ¼″ seam allowances. On pink fabric, trace 1 face, transferring facial features.
3. With 2 strands of floss, satin-stitch eyes green and cheeks pink. With 2 strands of red floss, satin-stitch nose and backstitch mouth. Cut out face, adding ¼″ seam allowance.
4. With right sides facing, stitch bottom of hat to top of beard, matching dots. Clip curves on face. Press seam allowance to wrong side. Pin face to beard and appliqué by hand.
5. Stack backing fabric, right side down; both pieces of quilt batting; and Santa, right side up. Machine-stitch on outline. Trim backing and batting even with Santa shape. Bind edges of pot holder with bias tape. With remaining bias tape, form a loop and stitch it to back of Santa's hat.

Christmas Pony Ornament

Materials
Pattern on page 145
6½" x 13" scrap of dark green print
2½" x 4" scrap from red bandanna
Thread to match
Polyester stuffing
Embroidery floss: dark green, black
Cardboard
8" (⅛"-wide) of silver soutache braid
3" (¼"-wide) of red grosgrain ribbon
8" of silver looped braid
6" of silver thread
Vanishing fabric marker

Instructions
1. Trace pattern pieces, transferring markings. Cut out.

2. Cut green fabric in half to make 2 (6½") squares. On wrong side of 1 square, use marker to trace pony and ear, transferring markings. *Do not cut out pieces yet.* With right sides facing, pin the 2 squares together. Set aside.

Trace saddle on right side of bandanna scrap, centering saddle on bandanna design. Cut out, adding ¼" seam allowance. Clip curves and finger-press seam allowance to wrong side.

3. Machine-stitch around pony and then ear, leaving openings as indicated. Cut out pieces, adding ¼" seam allowances. Clip curves and ear tips and turn. Stuff pony. *Do not stuff ear.* Slipstitch openings closed. Run row of gathering stitches across ear as indicated and gather. Wrap end of thread around ear piece 2 or 3 times and knot. Fold ear piece on gathering line to make 2 ears. Tack ears to top of head at dot.

4. To make mane, cut green embroidery floss into 3 (1-yard) lengths. Thread needle with 1 length. *Do not knot floss.* Take stitch into pony, entering at front edge of saddle area and exiting at base of neck seam. Take tiny lock stitch at point where needle exited. Take stitches at 1/16" intervals from base of neck to ears, making ½" loops and taking tiny lock stitches after each loop. Run needle under ears and add a few loops in front of ears. When out of floss, thread needle with second length and continue. To make tail, cut 1¾" square of cardboard. Wrap last length of floss around cardboard 6 times. Slip loops off and tack 1 end to pony where indicated.

5. With 1 strand of black embroidery floss, satin-stitch eyes. Tack center of soutache bridle above muzzle where indicated. Bring bridle around muzzle and tack underneath where indicated. Tack ends of bridle to back of neck.

Center ribbon under body and tack to body to form cinch strap. Sew looped braid around saddle. Place saddle on pony's back so that edges cover ends of bridle and cinch. Slipstitch saddle in place. Form loop with silver thread and tack to base of neck.

What a great way to use left-over bandanna scraps! This Christmas Pony Ornament will hang happily from a holiday tree or decorate a gift package with style.

Christmas Pony Sweatshirt

Materials
Pattern on page 145
Red sweatshirt
7″ square of dark green fabric
2″ square of red bandanna
Thread to match
5″ of silver looped braid
Embroidery floss: black, dark green
5″ (⅛″-wide) of silver soutache braid
2″ (¼″-wide) of red grosgrain ribbon
Vanishing fabric marker

Instructions
Note: Before beginning, wash and dry sweatshirt according to label.

1. Trace pony and ear patterns and bottom half of saddle below fold line, transferring markings. Cut out.

2. On right side of green fabric, use marker to trace pony, transferring markings. Cut out, adding ¼″ seam allowance. Clip curves and angles. Baste seam allowance to wrong side.

Cut remaining piece of green fabric in half. With right sides facing, baste pieces together around edges. Trace ear on fabric and machine-stitch outline, leaving opening as indicated. Cut out ear, adding ¼″ seam allowance. Clip curves and tips of ears and turn right side out. Slipstitch opening closed. Run a row of gathering stitches across ear and gather as indicated on pattern. Wrap end of thread around ear piece 2 or 3 times and knot. Fold on gathering line to make 2 ears.

Trace 1 saddle half on right side of bandanna scrap, and cut out, adding ¼″ seam allowance. Clip curves and finger-press seam allowance to wrong side. Stitch looped braid around curved edge of saddle. Using 1 strand of black floss, satin-stitch pony's eye.

3. Referring to photograph, center and pin pony to front of shirt. Slipstitch in place. Tack soutache braid across pony's muzzle. Tack other end to back of neck where end will be covered by saddle. Tack ribbon to pony's body below saddle to form cinch strap. Sew saddle in place, covering ends of bridle and cinch. Tack ear unit in place on pony's head.

4. Refer to Step 4 of Christmas Pony Ornament instructions, page 128, attaching mane and tail to sweatshirt.

Bandanna Boot Stockings

Materials for one stocking

Pattern on pages 146-147
Red bandanna with 3″ to 3½″ border and no center medallion
3 (11½″ x 15″) pieces of red fabric
Thread to match
2 (11½″ x 15″) pieces of quilt batting
53″ (¼″-wide) of dark green double-fold bias tape
Assorted silver braids, rickrack, jingle bells, sequins, and star appliqués
Vanishing fabric marker

Instructions

1. Trace stocking pattern, matching upper and lower sections to form 1 piece. Transfer markings and cut out.
2. Refer to border placement diagrams to determine pattern placement. (It may be necessary to cut bandanna and stitch 2 trimmed sections together to achieve look you want. Required seams to make second and third stockings from left in photograph are indicated on diagrams.)

On right side of bandanna, use marker to trace stocking shape, transferring markings. To make stocking front, stack 1 piece of red fabric, right side down; 1 piece of batting; and bandanna with stocking shape, right side up. Baste layers together. Cut out boot, adding 3/16″ seam allowance. Cut a 9¼″ piece of bias tape and bind top of stocking between Xs. Add trims as

desired (see photograph). Repeat to make stocking back, replacing bandanna with red fabric.

3. Pin front and back together with linings facing. Machine-stitch on outline, leaving top bound edges open between Xs. Beginning at X at top left of stocking (above toe), bind raw edges with bias tape, allowing tape to extend 5″ beyond X at top right of stocking (above heel). Fold extension to back of stocking, turn ends under ¼″, and tack to binding to form hanging loop. Add more trims, if desired (see photograph).

Stocking A

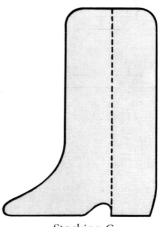

Stocking B

Stocking C

 Seam line

 Border

131

MINIATURE MAGIC

The delicate Filigree Heart Ornament and the mini-gift boxes may look intricate, but they're really quite simple—and speedy, too! So make dozens. Fill the boxes with candy to make sweet party favors, ornaments, gifts, or place cards.

Welcome Home Box

Materials
Pattern on page 148
5" x 8½" piece of red art paper
3½" square of white art paper
Scrap of green art paper
White glue
7" (⅛"-wide) of green ribbon
Craft knife
⅛" paper punch

Instructions
1. Trace pattern, transferring markings. Cut out.
2. From red paper, cut out 1 house. Transfer all pattern markings, except door and windows, to right side of house. Transfer markings for door and windows to wrong side of house. Use craft knife to lightly score fold lines. Cut out window within door placement lines on house. Cut other 2 windows on cutting lines and fold outward along fold lines to form the shutters.
3. From white paper cut 1 roof, transferring all markings, except glue area, to right side of roof. Transfer glue area to wrong side of roof. Cut 1 door from white paper, transferring marking for window. Cut out window on door. Cut chimney slit in roof and punch holes for ribbon hanger as indicated. Punch out door knob from green paper and glue in place as indicated. Glue door in place on house.
4. Fold house on all fold lines. Glue each of the 3 glue flaps on the floor and the flap to the left of the door in place on inside of house. Fold roof on fold line. Glue flap on top of house to roof where indicated. Let dry.
5. Thread 1 end of ribbon through each hole in roof and glue to inside of house at open circles. Insert chimney in chimney slit on roof.

Filigree Heart Ornament

Materials for three ornaments

Pattern on page 148
1 (4½″) square of green art paper
2 (4½″) squares of red art paper
Lightweight plastic template material
White glue
45″ (⅛″-wide) of ribbon for hangers
Craft knife
⅛″ paper punch

Instructions

1. Trace pattern on plastic template material. With craft knife, cut out on all lines.

2. Trace pattern on green square and both red squares of paper. To make red ornament pictured on this page, cut out heart and shell sections and center section from 1 red ornament. Cut out ornament on outer outline.

To make red-and-green ornament pictured on page 132, cut center section from second red ornament. Set aside. From green ornament, cut out heart and shell sections. Glue green cut-out hearts and shells in place on second red ornament. Cut out second red ornament on outer outline.

To make solid green ornament (not pictured), cut out center section from green ornament. Then cut out green ornament on outer outline.

3. Cut ribbon into 3 (15″) pieces. With 1 piece of ribbon, tie loop in 1 heart section of solid red ornament. Repeat for green ornament. Punch hole in top of red-and-green ornament as indicated on pattern and tie ribbon.

Paper Snowman Box and Paper Bear Box

Note: Using patterns for Snowman Box on page 149 and Bear Box on page 150, follow materials list and instructions for Paper Bunny Basket on page 39 to make a batch of charming Christmas gift boxes or ornaments.

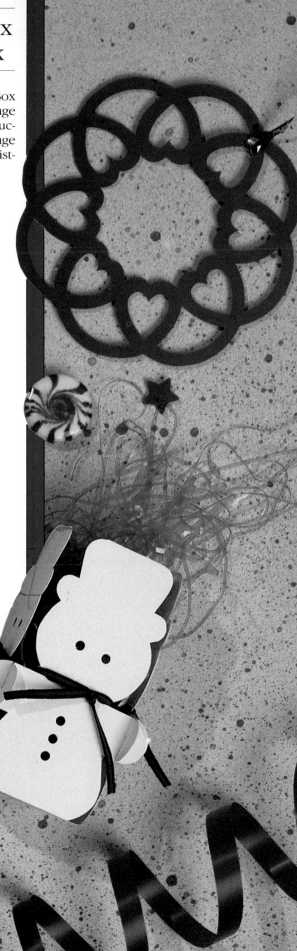

A TABLETOP TREAT

There's something for all skill levels in these festive paper projects. The Folded Paper Stars are so simple a child can make them. The Paper Tree takes a little more time, but it is almost as easy to make as its cousins, those paper lanterns you cut and pasted as a child. And while the Paper Bird requires a bit more skill than either the stars or the tree, the result—a graceful ornament that costs pennies to make—is worth the effort.

Paper Bird

Materials
Pattern on page 151
7½″ square of art paper
Transparent thread
Craft knife
⅛″ paper punch

Instructions
1. Trace pattern, transferring markings. Cut out.
2. Trace pattern on art paper. Transfer markings to backs of pieces. Cut out.
3. On body, use craft knife to lightly score the score lines and to cut 3 slots as indicated on pattern. Punch holes for eyes. On wings, lightly score only outermost score lines. Transfer center score line to reverse side of wing section. Lightly score with knife.
4. Bend body sides down along score lines. Insert tail in rear slot of body. Bend down outer wing sections along score lines. Bend up inner wing sections around center oval score line. Slip front of oval, at notch, into front

slot on body. Gently push wing section forward in slot so that oval rises and curves slightly. Insert wing tab into middle slot on body.
5. To make hanger, punch large pin hole at each X on wings. Run piece of transparent thread across oval section under bird, bringing thread ends up through holes on wings. Tie thread ends together above bird.

Paper Star Topper

Materials
Pattern on page 152
3″ x 6″ piece of colored art paper
Craft knife

Instructions
1. Trace pattern and cut out.
2. Using pattern, trace 2 star shapes on art paper. Cut out shapes.
3. Cut slits in both star shapes as indicated on pattern. Interlock stars through slits.

Look what can be made from a few sheets of art paper and some glue: bright stars in a variety of shapes, an easy-to-make tabletop tree trimmed with a fat red star, and a graceful bird in flight.

134

CHRISTMAS WINDOWS

A cozy Christmas window inspired these cheery place mat and pot holder designs. The appliqué and quilting are done by machine, so these projects are easier to make than they appear.

Place Mat

Materials
Pattern on page 153
9″ square of solid green fabric
9″ x 19″ piece of solid red fabric
12″ x 29″ piece of red-and-green miniprint fabric
10⅛″ (2″-wide) of white scalloped lace
12″ x 18″ piece of quilt batting
65″ (⅞″-wide) of white quilt binding
45″ (⅞″-wide) of red quilt binding
Thread to match
Red embroidery floss
40″ (½″-wide) of green rickrack
Vanishing fabric marker

Instructions

1. On folded paper, trace large wreath, transfer markings, and cut out.
2. From green fabric, cut 1 wreath, transferring bow placement line. From red fabric, cut 2 (18½″ x 4⅛″) rectangles for shutters. Using marker, mark pleat lines as indicated in Diagram 1. From miniprint, cut 1 (10⅛″ x 11⅜″) rectangle for window and 1 (12″ x 18″) rectangle for backing. (Dimensions include seam allowances.)
3. Pleat 1 shutter as indicated in Diagram 1. Fold on pleat line, bringing fold down to meet dotted line. Press. Repeat for all pleats. Baste pleats along seam allowance and press. Repeat for second shutter. Set aside.
4. With wrong side of lace facing right side of fabric, stitch lace across upper edge of window, with raw edges aligned and scallops pointing toward bottom of window.
5. With right sides facing, stitch 1 long edge of 1 pleated shutter to side of window. Repeat to attach second shutter. Press seams toward window.

With raw edges aligned, place batting on wrong side of backing. Center window, right side up, on batting. Baste layers together. Trim batting and lining to match window.
6. From white quilt binding, cut 3 (11⅜″) pieces and 1 (9⅝″) piece. Open center fold of each piece of binding and trim away ½″ along 1 edge to reduce bulk. Sew 9⅝″ piece of binding across center of window from side to side, topstitching close to each edge of binding through all layers. Sew 1 (11⅜″) piece of binding down center of window from top to bottom in same manner, stitching over lace and horizontal piece of binding. Sew 1 remaining 11⅜″ piece of binding to each side of window (but not on shutter) in same manner.
7. With 6 strands of floss, chainstitch bow. Clip inside and outside curves almost to seam lines. Turn seam allowances to wrong side and press.

Cut piece of rickrack the circumference of outside edge of wreath. On wrong side of wreath, center rickrack along outside edge so that half of rickrack extends beyond edge of fabric. Baste. Repeat for inside edge of wreath. Center wreath right side up on window and pin in place (see photograph). Machine-stitch around inner and outer edges of wreath.
8. Cut remaining white binding in half. Bind top and bottom of window from seam to seam, allowing ends to extend ¼″ beyond window frame onto shutter.
9. Cut red quilt binding in half. Tuck under ¼″ on each end of 1 piece of binding. Starting at top corner of window frame, place end of red binding over excess white binding and pin. Bind edges of 1 shutter, mitering binding at corners. Blindstitch edges of shutter binding to window binding. Repeat to bind other shutter.

Diagram 1: Place Mat Shutters

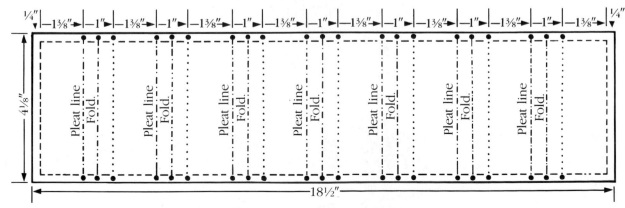

140

Bandanna
Boot Stockings

Instructions are on pages 130-131.

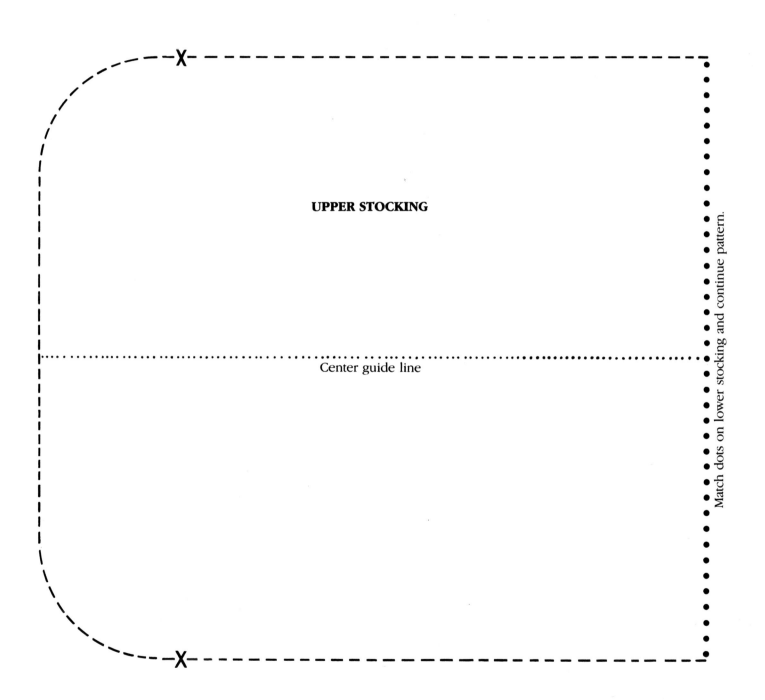

UPPER STOCKING

Center guide line

Match dots on lower stocking and continue pattern.

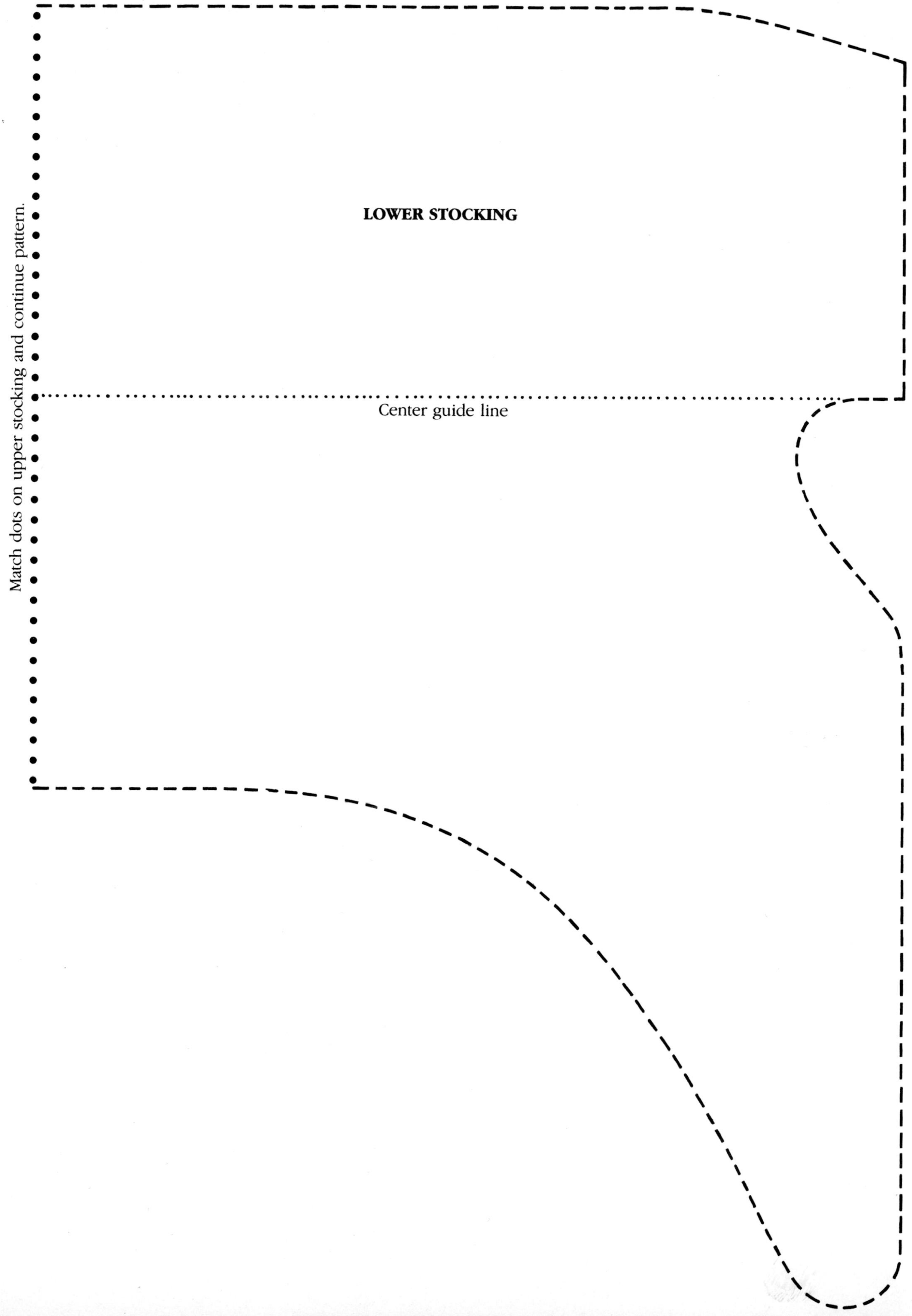

LOWER STOCKING

Match dots on upper stocking and continue pattern.

Center guide line

Welcome Home Box

Instructions are on page 132.

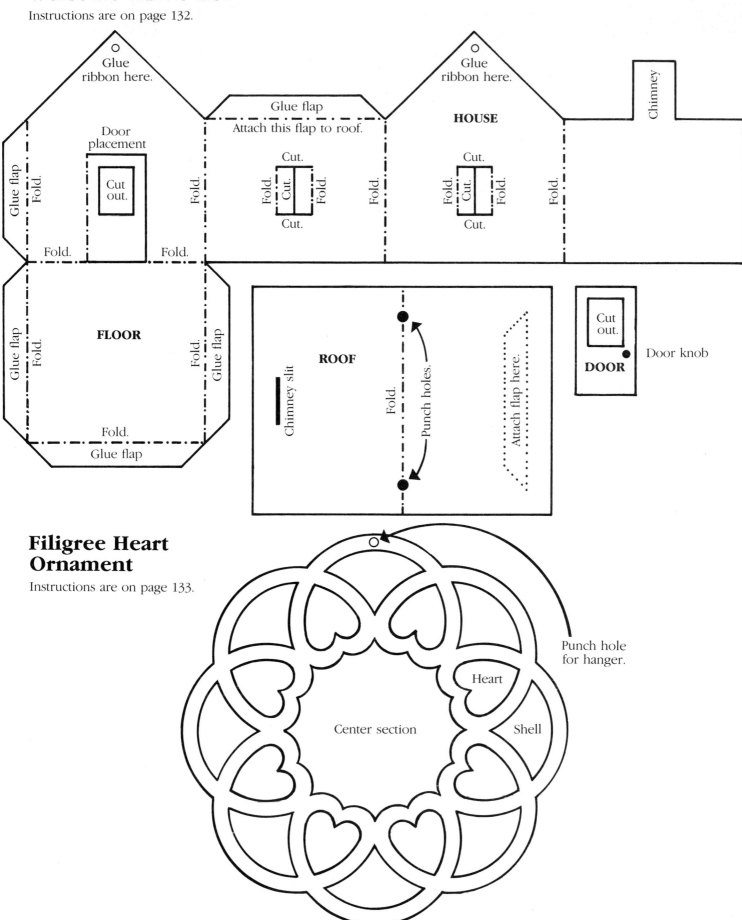

Glue ribbon here.

Door placement

Cut out.

Glue flap
Fold.

Fold.

Fold.

Glue flap
Fold.
FLOOR
Fold.
Glue flap

Fold.
Glue flap

Glue flap
Attach this flap to roof.

Cut.
Fold.
Cut.
Fold.
Cut.

Fold.

Glue ribbon here.

HOUSE

Cut.
Fold.
Cut.
Fold.
Cut.

Fold.

Chimney

Chimney slit

ROOF

Fold.

Punch holes.

Attach flap here.

Cut out.
DOOR

Door knob

Filigree Heart Ornament

Instructions are on page 133.

Punch hole for hanger.

Heart

Center section

Shell

Paper Snowman Box

Refer to instructions for Paper Bunny
Basket on page 39.

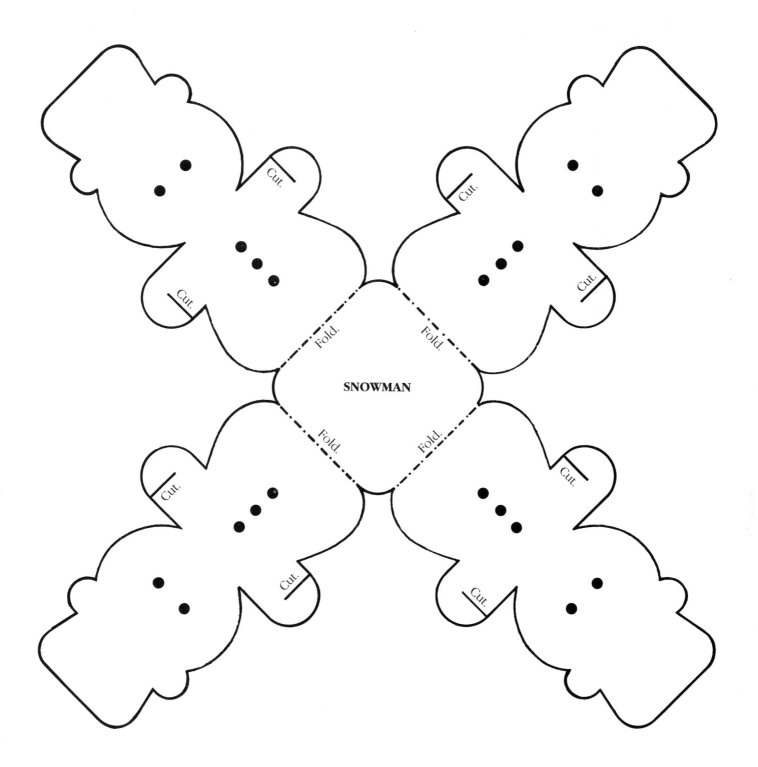

Paper Bear Box

Refer to instructions for Paper Bunny
Basket on page 39.

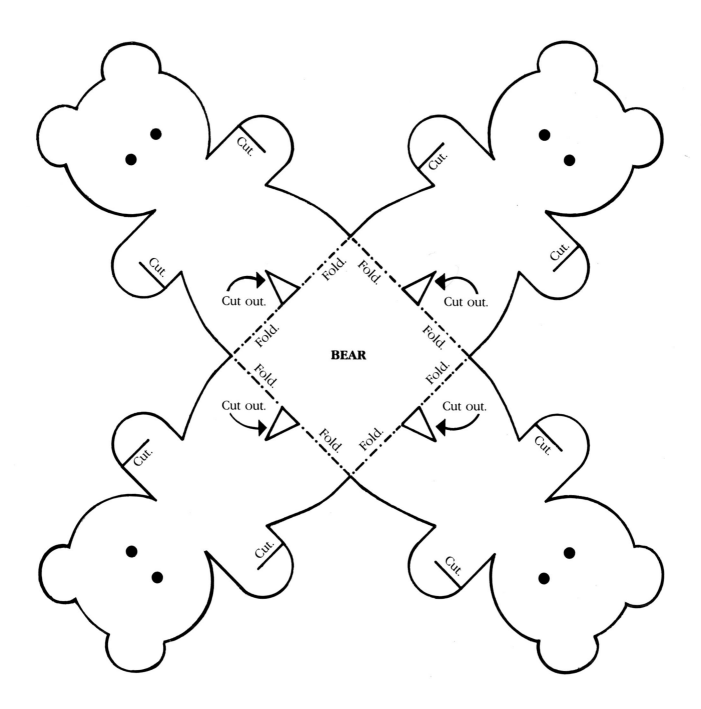

BEAR

Paper Bird

Instructions are on page 134.

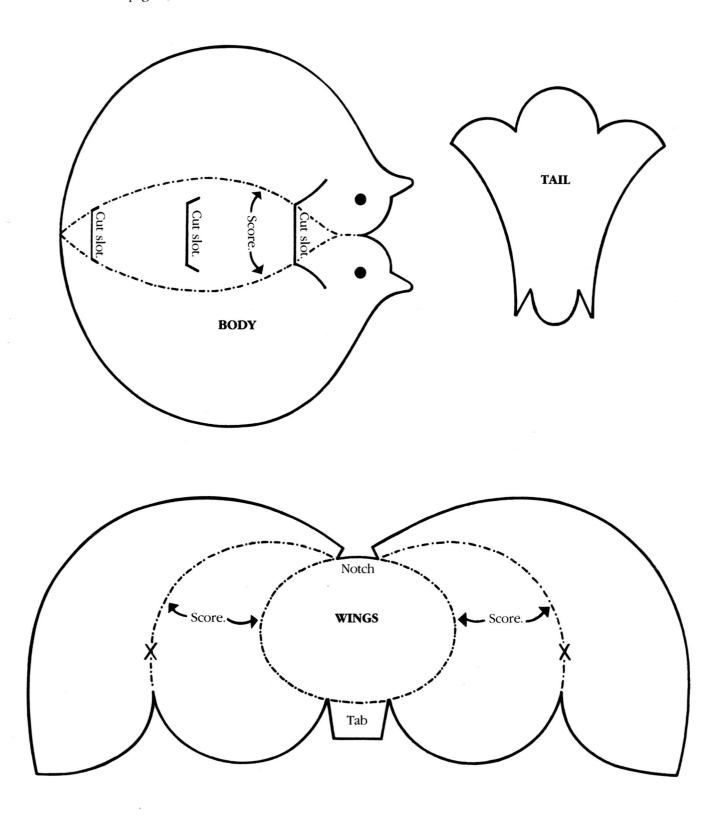

Cut slot.

Cut slot.

Score.

Cut slot.

BODY

TAIL

Notch

Score.

WINGS

Score.

Tab

Paper Star Topper

Instructions are on page 134.

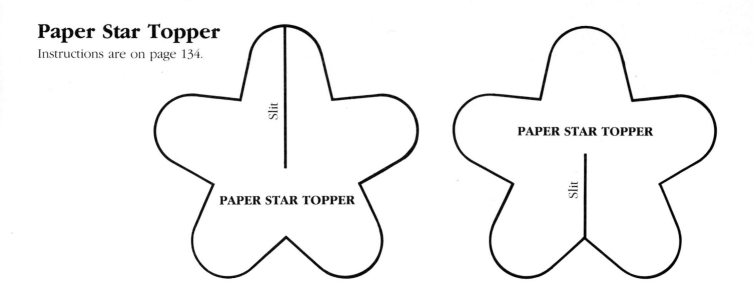

Luscious Lollipop Ornaments

Instructions are on pages 138-139.

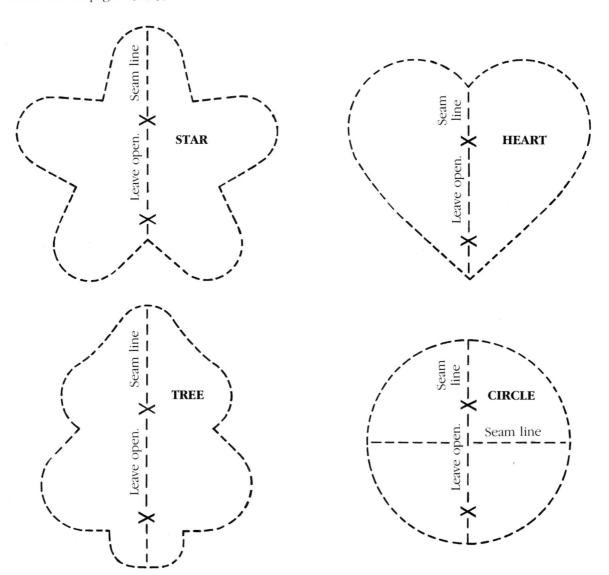

Christmas Windows
Place Mat

Instructions are on page 140.

Christmas Windows
Pot Holder

Instructions are on page 142.

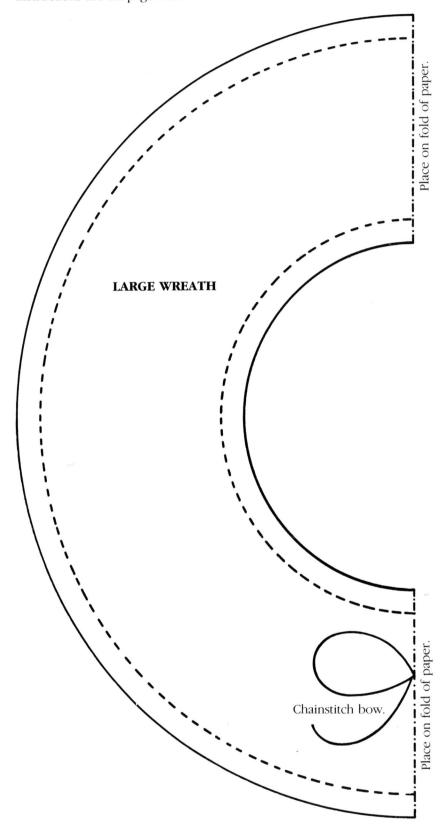

LARGE WREATH

Place on fold of paper.

Chainstitch bow.

Place on fold of paper.

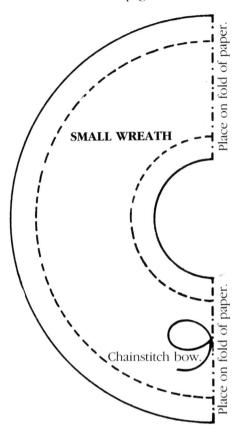

SMALL WREATH

Place on fold of paper.

Place on fold of paper.

Chainstitch bow.

SUPPLIES AND TECHNIQUES

Creative energy vanishes when you must search the house for your sewing supplies. For safety and sanity, keep these just-for-you items boxed together in a special hiding place.

Sewing Project Supplies

Scissors. Keep your sewing scissors sharp, and don't use them to cut paper. Use a 5″ pair of sewing scissors for general cutting. Embroidery scissors are perfect for trimming seam allowances and cutting out little pieces. You may also wish to have a pair of 7″ or 8″ lightweight sewing shears for larger projects. Pinking shears are handy for trimming seam allowances.

As an occasional alternate to scissors, a rotary cutter, used with a gridded self-healing mat and straightedge, provides a fast and easy way to cut multiple layers of fabric.

Craft knife. I prefer an X-acto® knife with a #11 blade. I use it to make patterns, and it's especially helpful for cutting out tiny details when making a template of a pattern. Practice using this tool, keeping the hand that is not holding the knife far away from the cutting line. Work slowly and do not press down. Wrap old blades before discarding.

Pattern materials. Use tracing paper to make most of the patterns. For making multiple projects, strengthen paper patterns by gluing them to thin cardboard or the smooth side of fine sandpaper. The textured side of the sandpaper will prevent the pattern from slipping when placed on fabric.

Graph paper is great for making quick straight-sided patterns. Purchase a pad with ⅛″ or ¼″ squares for this purpose.

Acetate is also a good material for making patterns. It can be purchased in sheets or saved from the tops of gift and stationery boxes. The plastic lids from coffee cans also make sturdy pattern material.

Measuring tools. I prefer a wide 15″ transparent plastic sewing ruler (often referred to as "the sewer's T square") and a fabric tape measure. Both of these can be purchased at fabric stores. Instead of a yardstick for making large patterns, I use a metal ruler as a cutting edge with the craft knife. These can be purchased at art supply stores.

Drawing tools. Use sharp #2 lead pencils on light fabric and white drawing pencils or tailor's chalk on dark fabric. Automatic pencils are a great boon. Because the tip never becomes dull, they're great for tracing around patterns and transferring dots.

Use a vanishing fabric marker, available in fabric stores, when it will be necessary to remove pattern markings. It looks just like a felt-tip pen, but its ink usually fades within 48 hours, and sometimes sooner. (Vanishing time varies according to the humidity. Fading takes especially long on some felt.) Always test the pen on a swatch of your fabric to make sure the ink will truly vanish.

Seam ripper. I hope you don't have to use it as often as I do, but you should have a seam ripper stashed away in your workbox. And here's a hint for using it: When you need to rip dark threads from dark fabric, first highlight the stitching line with tailor's chalk.

Tweezers. They're especially handy for pulling out threads as you're ripping out seams. At times, they also help me to thread the needle of my sewing machine.

Pins and needles. Rust- and corrosion-resistant pins are less likely to snag fabrics. I love extra-long super-strong quilting pins, but other sewers have different favorites. I prefer fine, small needles, about 1½″ long, for general sewing. But you'll need large-eyed, embroidery needles when using multiple stands of embroidery floss. An assortment pack of sewing machine needles is important, too, although you'll use numbers 11 and 14 most often.

When stitching by hand through sturdy fabrics, increase the needle power by first inserting the point into a bar of soap. Wearing a few cut-off fingers from an old rubber glove will help you pull the needle through thick batting.

Pin keepers. Although magnetic pin dispensers are a bit expensive, they're convenient and spillproof, and they're also helpful to locate stray pins. I use several pincushions or dispensers at once, placing one at the cutting area, one at the sewing machine, and one at the ironing board. Another neat pin keeper is an adhesive-backed magnetic strip that attaches to the flat surface of your sewing machine and attracts pins that wander too close to the needle or bobbin area.

Quilt batting. In most cases, use traditional-weight polyester batting. When necessary, however, you can substitute several thin layers for one thick layer. Purchase a crib-quilt-size piece for small projects and save the scraps for stuffing toys and pillows. If the batting is sold in a fat sausage shape, remove it from the plastic bag and unroll it at least a day before you plan to use it, allowing it to relax and let the wrinkles smooth out. A short tumble in a warm dryer will also help to diminish wrinkles.

Pressing equipment. Pressing is very important for successful sewing, so place your ironing board near the sewing machine, if possible. Be sure to keep the iron's sole plate clean. Check it often, especially after using fusible web.

A small tailor's ham isn't a necessity, but it's helpful when pressing curved seams. A pressing cloth is definitely a necessity, even if it's just a good-sized scrap of lightweight fabric.

Other helpful tools. There are a few more tools that will help you to work efficiently. Embroidery hoops are useful when doing decorative hand stitchery. A 3″- or 4″-diameter hoop is very handy for small projects, and an 8″-diameter hoop is also commonly used.

For turning and stuffing small pieces, try a crochet hook or a pencil with a blunted point (no lead showing). For larger work, use a wooden yardstick or a dowel. Once shapes are turned right side out, use a long sturdy needle to pull out corners and curves, but take care to avoid snagging the fabric.

Washable fabric glue is a great time-saver, and the thicker its consistency, the less it will soak through the fabric. Always apply the glue sparingly. A glue stick is useful for quick basting jobs. Always test the glue on a fabric swatch before applying it to a final project.

Allow the glue to dry thoroughly before you proceed with sewing.

Masking tape is a sewer's friend. When tracing patterns from a book, use it to anchor the tracing paper. (When you've finished tracing, the tape lifts off easily.) Masking tape can also be placed on the throat plate of your sewing machine to mark the seam allowance width. When you are machine-stitching a project that has a top layer of batting, the presser foot often catches the top fibers. To avoid this nuisance, wrap the "toes" of the presser foot together with a single piece of tape.

Fabrics. When yardages are given, it should be assumed that the fabrics are at least 44″ wide, unless otherwise specified. Lay out all the pattern pieces as close to each other as possible, but maintain enough space for seam allowances, if they need to be added.

Inspect fabrics carefully before you buy them and avoid those that fray easily. Use light- to medium-weight fabrics, unless others are suggested, and prewash them.

When the grain of the fabric is important to the design, grain lines are marked on the patterns, and you should lay out patterns accordingly. Since felt isn't woven, it doesn't have a grain, so you can place patterns freely. Because the iron heat and moisture can cause felt to shrink, steam away wrinkles before cutting felt. Most felt is not washable, but there is some beautiful washable felt available now. To keep it beautiful, I recommend gentle hand washing and line drying.

Sewing Project Techniques

Enlarging patterns. If a pattern is drawn on a grid, you can enlarge it as explained in Diagram 1. Instead of drawing multiple grids, make yourself a master grid: Draw 1″ squares (or the size required) on a large, sturdy piece of paper. Then tape tracing paper over the grid. Large sheets of graph paper can streamline this job even more. If you have a folding cardboard cutting surface, ruled in 1″ squares, it can also be used as a 1″ master grid. When opened, the cardboard provides a large work area that protects your

table or floor, and you can stick pins right into it to anchor your drawings and fabrics.

Diagram 1: Enlarging a pattern

Rule a piece of tracing paper with a grid of squares the size required in the directions for the project. Carefully copy the original pattern square by square. Each square in your enlargement should contain the same portion and shape shown in each square of the original.

Making patterns. Draw neat and accurate patterns, copying all the matching dots and embroidery and placement lines, and labeling each piece. (Photocopiers usually distort or reduce patterns ever so slightly. For this reason, they should be avoided for pattern making.)

Because of space limitations, frequently only one half of a pattern has been drawn in this book. To make a complete pattern, trace these half patterns on folded tracing paper, transferring markings to both right and left sides. Half patterns in this book are not meant to be placed on folded fabric unless otherwise indicated.

Read the directions for each project before you trace the patterns and determine whether the seam allowances are included or must be added. Solid pattern lines indicate cutting lines for fabrics and felt, broken lines indicate stitching lines, fine dotted lines indicate placement lines, and alternating broken and dotted lines indicate fold lines.

I frequently cut quilt patterns from

acetate and then, using nail polish, I label them and paint a thin layer of color around the edges. This outlining makes it easier to center the transparent patterns on the fabric motifs. It also helps me to locate the patterns quickly. Because of the painted label, I can also tell at a glance when the pattern is reversed.

Marking fabrics. Unless otherwise instructed, place the pattern face down on the wrong side of the fabric, hold or pin it in place, and draw around it with a sharp #2 lead pencil.

When drawing small pattern pieces on fabrics, first place an 8½″ x 11″ piece of fine-textured sandpaper on your work surface. With this base, the fabric will not be pulled as much when you draw around the patterns.

Transferring markings. There are several ways to transfer embroidery or placement lines to the right side of the fabric.

1. You can make a stencil of some patterns, such as those for facial features, by cutting out the details. Center the pattern on the front of the cutout fabric shape and draw the details, using very light pencil strokes or a vanishing fabric marker. Or draw the details on the back of the fabric and transfer them to the front with tiny basting stitches.

2. To transfer details using the rub-off technique, go over the details on the back of the patterns with a sharp #2 lead pencil. Center the pattern on the front of the fabric piece, and then rub off the design with a flat wooden stick or a similar burnisher. This can get a little messy.

3. A sunny window can also be used to transfer pattern details. Tape the pattern to the wrong side of a piece of fabric of manageable size, and trace the pattern outline. Then tape the fabric and pattern to the window, pattern against the glass, and lightly trace the details onto the right side of the fabric.

4. When transferring details to felt, use the following method: Instead of making a template of the pattern, use a large needle to make holes along the pattern lines. Hold the pattern against the felt shape and carefully mark through the holes with a sharp pencil.

5. When I embroider facial details on a stuffed toy, I often draw the features with a vanishing fabric marker after the head is stuffed. Since filling can distort the face considerably, I wait until after the head is formed to find the best position for the face.

Whatever method you use, draw lightly. Once you've marked the right side of the fabric, do not iron over the drawing, because the heat may set the lines permanently, even those made with a vanishing marker.

Stitching and trimming seams. Although shortcuts are tempting, it's really best to pin and baste your fabric pieces together before stitching them. If there are dots to be matched, line up the pieces, right sides together, and push a pin straight down through both fabric layers at the dots. Then pin along the seam allowance, but not on the seam line, perpendicular to the edge. Baste, remove pins, and then machine-stitch the seams.

I don't advise sewing over pins. There's too much chance of injuring your machine or yourself!

Grading seam allowances. To make seams smooth on the right side, bulky seam allowances (those involving several layers of fabric or batting) should be graded. Cut each layer of the seam allowance a different distance from the stitching line. For instance, if a seam allowance is ½″ wide, trim the bottom layer to ⅜″ and the top layer to ¼″. Always cut across corners, trimming close to the stitching. Make vertical clips in the seam allowance on curves, clipping almost to the stitching line.

Gathering. When making long machine stitches that will be gathered, two closely placed rows of stitches, ⅛″ apart, are better than one. If you use different colors for the top and bobbin threads, it will be easy to identify the bobbin thread to pull for gathering.

Applying bias tape. Before binding an edge with bias tape, trim seam allowance so that it is about ¹⁄₁₆″ narrower than the bias tape. If seam allowances are very thick, zigzag-stitch edges to flatten. Clip into any angles around the shape.

When using double-fold bias tape or quilt binding as a flat trim, use the following method: Open the center fold of the tape and trim away one folded edge ⅛″ or more from the center fold. Discard the trimming.

Mitering bias tape. Refer to the illustrations and the instructions in Diagram 2.

Quilting. When batting is sandwiched between two pieces of fabric, the layers must be pinned and basted together so that they won't shift. Work from the center to the outside of the piece, making 1″ stitches horizontally, vertically, and diagonally across the piece. To quilt, use a short quilting needle and make uniform running stitches through all layers. Gather several stitches on your needle before pulling the thread through the fabric. Quilting stitches are usually placed ¼″ from the seam line, but I sometimes quilt right on the seam line, "in the ditch." For machine-quilting, use long straight stitches.

Adding appliqués. If you plan to handstitch an appliqué, the piece must be cut with a hem allowance. For the best results, make tiny basting stitches along the outline of the appliqué shape, to create a precise folding edge for the hem. To make the hemming of small pieces easier, cut them out with pinking shears or clip hem allowances at close intervals. Turn under the hem allowance and baste. Pin and baste the shape in place and appliqué it invisibly with slipstitches, or blanket-stitch the edge of the shape.

If you intend to attach an appliqué with machine zigzag stitches, it need not be cut with a hem allowance. To secure the appliqué before stitching, use fusible web to attach it to the fabric and then stitch with very close zigzag stitches.

Stuffing and such. Polyester stuffing is easiest to work with. Keep it clean and free of thread and fabric clippings.

It's best to add stuffing in small quantities. When filling a doll or an animal, start with the smaller parts, such as the arms, legs, and head. Really pack in the stuffing, with the aid of a crochet hook, blunt pencil, or a wooden spoon handle. Have an extra bag of stuffing on hand. You'll almost always need more than you expect. (Most projects need to be firmly stuffed, although occasionally a project will require a flat, softly stuffed appearance.) You can mold the item with your hands as you stuff it.

Some words of caution. Please don't add buttons, bells, pom-poms, or similar embellishments to gifts that will go to households with very young children. Heed my advice if I suggest that a certain design is not intended to be a plaything. There are lots of gifts for little ones in this book, so choose the safe ones and stitch them securely, using prewashed materials.

Diagram 2: Mitering bias tape used as a binding

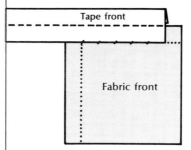

Figure A: Open center fold of tape and place one edge of tape along placement line. Slipstitch tape to front of fabric.

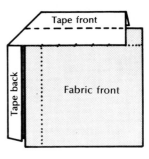

Figure B: At the corner, fold the loose end of the tape toward wrong side of the fabric at a 45-degree angle.

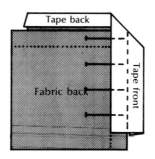

Figure C: Turn the work over and pin the tape along placement line, as shown.

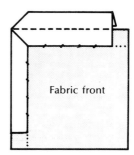

Figure D: Turn the work to the right side. Fold the flap of pinned tape toward the right side and slipstitch to fabric.

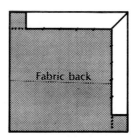

Figure E: Turn the work to the wrong side, fold down the remaining tape, and pin in position. Slipstitch the tape to wrong side of fabric.

Paper Project Supplies

Paper. To assure best results, use sturdy, high-quality paper such as Canson or Crescent when making the paper projects in this book. These richly hued papers can be found in art supply stores. Or consider colored paper used for pastel drawings and watercolors. Some large photocopy stores offer beautifully colored heavyweight paper for sale by the sheet. Don't be tempted to substitute construction paper. It often splits when scored and folded, and it won't withstand the handling that many of the paper projects require.

Cutting tools. You'll need a cutting board or a piece of heavy cardboard (not corrugated) to protect your work surface. I prefer an X-acto® knife with a new #11 blade for cutting and scoring. Keep an extra supply of blades on hand. Dull blades make ragged, inaccurate cuts. Standard ¼" and ⅛" paper punches are frequently used for paper projects in this book.

Paper Project Techniques

Making patterns. Accuracy is essential when drawing and cutting patterns for paper projects. I usually discourage the use of a photocopier when copying patterns for fabric projects. But it's an efficient way to copy paper project patterns. Photocopy the pattern directly from the book, glue the photocopy to lightweight cardboard or plastic if you wish, and cut out the pattern.

If no photocopier is available, trace the pattern and markings onto tracing paper, glue the tracing paper to cardboard or plastic, and cut out the pattern on the outline.

Marking paper. Transfer patterns to art paper with a sharp #2 lead pencil. Score fold lines by lightly drawing the craft knife blade over the fold line.

Other hints. To increase the art paper's flexibility on pieces that will be curved, such as bows and basket handles, gently pull the piece over a table edge or scissors blade. The paper will curl slightly, making it easier to bend into shape.

To keep hands free for other tasks, hold glued areas of paper projects together for drying with paper clips or clip clothes pins.

Embroidery Stitches

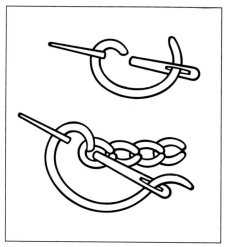

Chain stitch. Working from right to left, or top to bottom, depending on your preference, bring the needle up and make a loop with the thread. Holding the loop against the fabric, insert the needle again, as close as possible to where the thread last emerged. Take a short stitch over the looped thread, to anchor it.

French knot. Bring the needle up where you want an embroidered dot. Wrap the thread several times around the point of the needle. Insert the needle again as close as possible to the spot where the thread emerged. Holding the wraps in place, pull the thread to the wrong side.

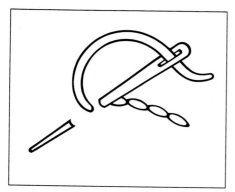

Backstitch. Working from right to left, bring the needle up on the guideline. Take a stitch backward and bring the needle up an equal distance ahead of the first hole made by thread. Repeat, taking the needle back to the end of the previous stitch.

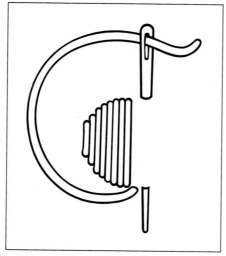

Satin stitch. Working from one end of a figure to the other, bring the needle up on one side and insert it on the opposite side. Carrying the thread behind the work, repeat from side to side, keeping the stitches parallel, smooth, and close together.

Lazy daisy stitch. Make a chain-stitch loop; then insert the needle to anchor the end of the loop and bring the needle up at the beginning of the next loop.

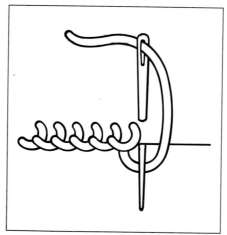

Blanket stitch. This is a stitch for edge-finishing. Bring the needle out along the edge of the fabric. Insert the needle above and to the right of the starting point and bring it out in line with the last stitch on the fabric edge, keeping the thread behind the needle point. Continue working from left to right and top to bottom.

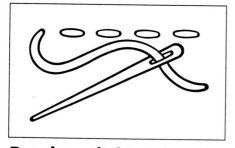

Running stitch. Working from right to left, make stitches of the same size, with even spaces between them. Use running stitches for quilting, gathering several stitches on the needle before pulling the thread through the fabric.

Special thanks to C.M. Offray & Son, Inc., for sharing ribbons and to Coats & Clark for supplying Coats Rickrack and Coats Bias Tape.